Test Prep & Admissions Consulting

Turbocharge Your GMAT
Verbal Study Guide

5th Edition (December 18th, 2012)

- □ *GMAT in a Nutshell*
- □ *Grammar Review*
- □ *Sentence Correction Guide*
- □ *Critical Reasoning Framework*
- □ *Reading Comprehension Strategies*
- □ *Basic to Advanced Content*
- □ *Free Web Downloads Available*

www.manhattanreview.com

Copyright and Terms of Use

10-Digit International Standard Book Number: (ISBN: 1629260150)
13-Digit International Standard Book Number: (ISBN: 978-1-62926-015-0)

Last updated on December 18, 2012.

Manhattan Review, 275 Madison Avenue, Suite 424, New York, NY 10025.
Phone: +1 (212) 316-2000. E-Mail: info@manhattanreview.com. Web: www.manhattanreview.com

About the Turbocharge your GMAT Series [5th Edition]

The highly acclaimed Turbocharge Your GMAT series is the result of the arduous effort of Manhattan Review to offer the most comprehensive and clear treatment of the concepts tested in the GMAT. The Manhattan Review Turbocharge Your GMAT preparation materials include over 600 pages of well-illustrated and professionally presented strategies and originally written problems for both the Verbal Section and Quantitative Section, 200 pages of detailed solutions, and more than 300 pages of internally developed Quantitative Glossary and Verbal Vocabulary List with detailed definitions, related words and sentence examples. The detailed breakdown of exclusive practice problems per category is 40+ Reading Comprehension passages, 60 Critical Reasoning questions, 250 Sentence Correction questions, and 300+ Quantitative questions.

Manhattan Review uses this material when delivering its weekend crash courses, one-week intensive courses, weekday and weekend long courses, online workshops, free seminars, and private tutoring to students in the US, UK, Continental Europe, Asia and the rest of the world. Please visit www.manhattanreview.com to find out more and also take a free GMAT practice test!

- ☐ **GMAT Math Study Guide (ISBN: 978-1-62926-013-6)**
- ☐ **GMAT Math Study Companion (ISBN: 978-1-62926-014-3)**
- ■ **GMAT Verbal Study Guide (ISBN: 978-1-62926-015-0)**
- ☐ **GMAT Verbal Study Companion (ISBN: 978-1-62926-016-7)**
- ☐ **GMAT Math Essentials (ISBN: 978-1-62926-017-4)**
- ☐ **GMAT Algebra (ISBN: 978-1-62926-018-1)**
- ☐ **GMAT Geometry (ISBN: 978-1-62926-019-8)**
- ☐ **GMAT Word Problems & Statistics (ISBN: 978-1-62926-020-4)**
- ☐ **GMAT Combinatorics & Probability (ISBN: 978-1-62926-021-1)**
- ☐ **GMAT Sentence Correction Guide (ISBN: 978-1-62926-022-8)**
- ☐ **GMAT Critical Reasoning Guide (ISBN: 978-1-62926-023-5)**
- ☐ **GMAT Reading Comprehension Guide (ISBN: 978-1-62926-024-2)**
- ☐ **GMAT Integrated Reasoning Guide (ISBN: 978-1-62926-025-9)**
- ☐ **GMAT Vocabulary Builder (ISBN: 978-1-62926-026-6)**

About the Company

Manhattan Review's origin can be traced directly to an Ivy-League MBA classroom in 1999. While lecturing on advanced quantitative subjects to MBAs at Columbia Business School in New York City, Prof. Dr. Joern Meissner was asked by his students to assist their friends, who were frustrated with conventional GMAT preparation options. He started to create original lectures that focused on presenting the GMAT content in a coherent and concise manner rather than a download of voluminous basic knowledge interspersed with so-called "tricks." The new approach immediately proved highly popular with GMAT students, inspiring the birth of Manhattan Review. Over the past 15+ years, Manhattan Review has grown into a multi-national firm, focusing on GMAT, GRE, LSAT, SAT, and TOEFL test prep and tutoring, along with business school, graduate school and college admissions consulting, application advisory and essay editing services.

About the Founder

Professor Joern Meissner, the founder and chairman of Manhattan Review has over twenty-five years of teaching experience in undergraduate and graduate programs at prestigious business schools in the USA, UK and Germany. He created the original lectures, which are constantly updated by the Manhattan Review Team to reflect the evolving nature of the GMAT GRE, LSAT, SAT, and TOEFL test prep and private tutoring. Professor Meissner received his Ph.D. in Management Science from Graduate School of Business at Columbia University (Columbia Business School) in New York City and is a recognized authority in the area of Supply Chain Management (SCM), Dynamic Pricing and Revenue Management. Currently, he holds the position of Full Professor of Supply Chain Management and Pricing Strategy at Kuehne Logistics University in Hamburg, Germany. Professor Meissner is a passionate and enthusiastic teacher. He believes that grasping an idea is only half of the fun; conveying it to others makes it whole. At his previous position at Lancaster University Management School, he taught the MBA Core course in Operations Management and originated three new MBA Electives: Advanced Decision Models, Supply Chain Management, and Revenue Management. He has also lectured at the University of Hamburg, the Leipzig Graduate School of Management (HHL), and the University of Mannheim. Professor Meissner offers a variety of Executive Education courses aimed at business professionals, managers, leaders, and executives who strive for professional and personal growth. He frequently advises companies ranging from Fortune 500 companies to emerging start-ups on various issues related to his research expertise. Please visit his academic homepage www.meiss.com for further information.

Manhattan Review Advantages

▶ **Time Efficiency and Cost Effectiveness**

- The most limiting factor in test preparation for most people is time.
- It takes significantly more teaching experience and techniques to prepare a student in less time.
- Our preparation is tailored for busy professionals. We will teach you what you need to know in the least amount of time.

▶ **High-quality and dedicated instructors who are committed to helping every student reach her/his goals**

▶ **Manhattan Review's team members have combined wisdom of**

- Academic achievements
- MBA teaching experience at prestigious business schools in the US and UK
- Career success

▶ **Our curriculum & proprietary Turbocharge Your GMAT course materials**

- About 600 pages of well-illustrated and professionally presented strategies and exclusive problems for both the Verbal and the Quantitative Sections
- 200+ pages of detailed solutions
- 300-page of internally developed Quantitative and Verbal vocabulary list with detailed definitions, related words and sentence examples
- Challenging Online CATs (Included in any course payments; Available for separate purchases)

▶ **Combine with Private Tutoring for an individually tailored study package**

▶ **Special Offer for Our Online Recording Library (Visit Online Library on our website)**

▶ **High-quality Career, MBA & College Advisory Full Service**

▶ **Our Pursuit of Excellence in All Areas of Our Service**

Visit us often at www.ManhattanReview.com.
(Select International Locations for your local content!)

International Phone Numbers & Official Manhattan Review Websites

Manhattan Headquarters	+1-212-316-2000	www.manhattanreview.com
USA & Canada	+1-800-246-4600	www.manhattanreview.com
Australia	+61-3-9001-6618	www.manhattanreview.com
Austria	+43-720-115-549	www.review.at
Belgium	+32-2-808-5163	www.manhattanreview.be
China	+86-20-2910-1913	www.manhattanreview.cn
Czech Republic	+1-212-316-2000	www.review.cz
France	+33-1-8488-4204	www.review.fr
Germany	+49-89-3803-8856	www.review.de
Greece	+1-212-316-2000	www.review.com.gr
Hong Kong	+852-5808-2704	www.review.hk
Hungary	+1-212-316-2000	www.review.co.hu
India	+1-212-316-2000	www.review.in
Indonesia	+1-212-316-2000	www.manhattanreview.com
Ireland	+1-212-316-2000	www.gmat.ie
Italy	+39-06-9338-7617	www.manhattanreview.it
Japan	+81-3-4589-5125	www.manhattanreview.jp
Malaysia	+1-212-316-2000	www.manhattanreview.com
Netherlands	+31-20-808-4399	www.manhattanreview.nl
Philippines	+1-212-316-2000	www.review.ph
Poland	+1-212-316-2000	www.review.pl
Portugal	+1-212-316-2000	www.review.pt
Russia	+1-212-316-2000	www.manhattanreview.ru
Singapore	+65-3158-2571	www.gmat.sg
South Africa	+1-212-316-2000	www.manhattanreview.co.za
South Korea	+1-212-316-2000	www.manhattanreview.kr
Sweden	+1-212-316-2000	www.gmat.se
Spain	+34-911-876-504	www.review.es
Switzerland	+41-435-080-991	www.review.ch
Taiwan	+1-212-316-2000	www.gmat.tw
Thailand	+66-6-0003-5529	www.manhattanreview.com
United Arab Emirates	+1-212-316-2000	www.manhattanreview.ae
United Kingdom	+44-20-7060-9800	www.manhattanreview.co.uk
Rest of World	+1-212-316-2000	www.manhattanreview.com

Contents

Chapter 1

GMAT in a Nutshell

1.1 Overview of GMAT

Business School applicants must take the Graduate Management Admissions Test (GMAT). The GMAT is a standardized test delivered in English. Unlike academic grades, which have varying significance based on each school's grading guidelines, the GMAT scores are based on the same standard for all test takers and they help business schools assess the qualification of an individual against a large pool of applicants with diverse personal and professional backgrounds. The GMAT scores play a significant role in admissions decisions since they are more recent than most academic transcripts of an applicant and they evaluate a person's verbal, quantitative and writing skills.

The GMAT is approximately 4-hour Computer Adaptive Test (CAT) and can be taken at any one of many test centers around the world 5 or 6 days a week. You may take the GMAT only once every 31 days and no more than five times within any 12-month period. The retest policy applies even if you cancel your score within that time period. All of your scores and cancellations within the last five years will be reported to the institutions you designate as score recipients.

The GMAT consists of three separately timed sections. GMAT has changed in June 2012. Before June '12, there used to be two 30-minute sub-sections consists of an analytical writing task of writing an Argument essay, also known as Analytical Writing Assessment (AWA). After June 2012, there is only one analytical writing task. The second AWA task, an issue based essay, is changed to Integrated Reasoning section. The remaining two 75-minute sections (Quantitative and Verbal) consist of multiple-choice questions delivered in a computer-adaptive format. Questions in these sections are dynamically selected as you take the test to stay commensurate with your ability level. Therefore, your test will be unique. Just one question is shown on the screen at a given time. However, Integrated Reasoning is not computer-adaptive section. It is impossible to skip a question or go back to a prior question in any section. Each problem needs to be answered before the next question.

In both the Verbal and Math sections, everyone starts out with an average difficulty level. The difficulty of subsequent questions then increases or decreases based on the correct or incorrect answers a person submits in the test. For each correct answer you give, you are given a harder question for each subsequent question and for each incorrect answer you are given an easier question. This process will continue until you finish the section, at which point the computer will have an accurate assessment of your ability level in that subject area.

Your score is determined by three factors: 1) the number of questions you complete; 2) the number of questions you answer correctly and; 3) the level of difficulty and other statistical characteristics of each question. To derive a final score, these questions are weighted based on their difficulty and other statistical properties, not their position in the test.

For the AWA section, one person and one computer programmed for grading (E-rater) score the essay based on essay content, organization, grammar and syntactic variety. Your final, single score is an average of both individual cores obtained on the argument essay. In the Integrated Reasoning section, there are 12 questions. The IR score range from 1-8 with an an interval of 1 point. AWA score and Integrated Reasoning score are computed separately from other sections and have no effect on the Verbal, Quantitative, or Total score.

The scores necessary to get into top schools are increasing year by year. Studies indicate that applicants who prepare for the GMAT score substantially higher than those who don't. In addition to the admissions process, GMAT scores are also considered in job recruitments and scholarship awards. A good GMAT score can save you thousands of dollars in tuition. Disciplined and dedicated preparation for the GMAT will allow you to get the best score possible on the exam and get into the school of your choice.

Although the GMAT score is considered as a reasonable indicator of future academic performance at business schools, it does not measure your job performance, knowledge of business, interpersonal skills, and personality traits such as motivation and creativity. Instead, your application, essays, recommendation letters and interviews will capture most of those aspects.

Student Notes:

1.1.1   2012 Changes in Test Administration

As stated earlier that in the year 2012, GMAC has ushered in a major change in the test content of the GMAT with the introduction of Integrated Reasoning sub-section in place of Issue based essay AWA task.

Since year 2006, Pearson VUE administering the GMAT, but GMAC, the owner of the

GMAT, will still be responsible for setting the standards for the exam itself including format, question types, difficulty levels, adaptive design, etc.

This partnership between the GMAC and Pearson VUE provides:

- A broader test center network (more than 400 locations in nearly 82 countries) with biometrically enhanced equipment

- On-line score report which ensures a reliable, timely, and efficient approach to both test takers and admissions offices (Hard copy of score report is available upon request)

- Improved overall customer service, in particular, secure on-line test registration worldwide

We have summarized and prioritized the key changes affecting the test taker as follows:

You can take the GMAT only ONCE every 31 days.

The old rule allowed people to take the exam first on March 31st and again on April 1st, as the criterion was "once per calendar month". Now you are permitted to take the test only once every 31 days.

Though we generally recommend our students to ace the test on their first try, it is wise to leave yourself some scheduling flexibility for a second attempt if necessary. Schedule your GMAT 5 to 6 weeks prior to your application deadline.

A note: If you receive a perfect score of 800, you may not retake the exam for 5 years.

Replacement of Scratch Paper with note-board or booklet with 5 sheets

You cannot skip AWA and IR, and must complete the entire test.
No longer will you be permitted to ignore the essay section of the test. You must take the test in its set order and in its entirety, **including the essay section**, or your scores will not be processed.
All scores and cancellations in the past 5 years will be on your score report.

No longer will only your last 3 scores/cancellations be noted on your score report, but all of the scores you received or cancelled in the last 5 years will be noted on your score report.

We recommend you only cancel your score if you are sure that your performance is not indicative of your normal and true ability, due to unusual reasons such as health, emotions, accident, disturbing testing environment, etc. By canceling the score, you avoid showing an inconsistency of your test performance which might be a red flag for admissions officers.

Otherwise, you should get your score so that you can get an objective evaluation of what you stand against other GMAT test takers and your strengths and weaknesses. As long as you demonstrate consistent and improved test results, reporting the score is generally preferred over cancellation.

You will receive your official score report on-line via an email notification 20 days after test day. Paper score report will be available via mail upon request only.

Based on our students' experience, it takes exactly 20 days for them to receive an email notification. You will still receive an unofficial copy of your scores immediately after completing the exam and prior to leaving the testing center. Typically you may fax or bring in a copy of the unofficial GMAT score report to be used to process your MBA application until the official scores arrive from the testing services. MBA programs usually can use the unofficial score report to make a recommendation on an application, but the official GMAT scores must reach the school before an official offer of admission can be made.

1.1.2 GMAT Sections and Score Distributions

The GMAT includes the following sections:

Math Section	*Verbal Section*	*Essay & IR Section*
• Problem Solving	• Sentence Correction	• Analytical Writing Assessment
• Data Sufficiency	• Critical Reasoning	• Integrated Reasoning
	• Reading Comprehension	

Each section requires its own specific strategy, but you may apply some techniques to all sections.

Please note that not all of the IR, verbal and quantitative questions are scored. In the Verbal section, approximately 37 of the 41 questions are scored, and in the quantitative section, approximately 33 of the 37 questions are scored. The number of unsecured questions for IR may be one to three; there is no verified information available so far. The un-scored questions are there for the purpose of gauging results for future tests.

Section	No. of Questions	Time Allowed	Details	Raw Score
•AWA	1	30 min	• Analysis of an Argument (30 min., 1 topic)	0 - 6
No Break! •IR	12	30 min	• Integrated Reasoning (12 questions)	1-8
Optional Break of 8 minutes		8 min		
•Math	37	75 min	• Problem Solving (23-24 questions) • Data Sufficiency (13-14 questions) Total number of questions: 37	0 - 60
Optional Break of 8 minutes		8 min		
•Verbal	41	75 min	• Critical Reasoning (14-15 questions) • Sentence Correction (14-15 questions) • Reading Comprehension (4 passages, 12-14 questions) Total number of questions: 41	0 - 60
Total Time		**4 hours (approx.)**		Scaled Score: 200 - 800

Note: The Integrated Reasoning sub-section will follow AWA task (The Argument essay).

GMAT scaled scores range from 200 to 800, which is the main score for you. It is measured in the interval of 10 points with an Standard Error of 30-40 points. About 66 % of test takers score between 400 and 600. The Verbal and Quantitative sections raw scores range from 0 to 60. It is measured in the interval of 1 points.

For GMAT Total score, most people score between 500 and 600. In a sample of 8000,000 candidates, mean scaled Score for GMAT is 545.6 with a Standard Deviation of 121.

For the AWA sub-section, most people score between 3 and 5. In a sample of 270,000 candidates, mean Raw Score for AWA is 4.3 with a Standard Deviation of 1.17.

For the IR sub-section, most people score between 3 and 7. In a sample of 200,000 candidates, mean Raw Score for IR is 4.34 with a Standard Deviation of 2.10.

For the Verbal section, most people score between 9 and 44. In a sample of 800,000 candidates, mean Raw Score for Verbal is 27.3 with a Standard Deviation of 9.12.

For the Quantitative section, common scores are between 7 and 50. In a sample of 800,000 candidates, mean Raw Score for Quants is 37.3 with a Standard Deviation of 11.

The Verbal and Quantitative scores measure different things and cannot be compared to each other, however, each section's score can be compared across different GMAT tests.

Your GMAT score is an important part of your overall application.

- If you receive a score below 500, we recommend that you retake the exam. A score below 500 will likely make acceptance to any school rather difficult.

- A score below 600 will make acceptance into a top school unlikely without an otherwise flawless application.

- A score in the range of 600-700 will help keep you in the running for acceptance into a top business school.

- A score above 700 is terrific and will help improve your MBA applications.

- Scaled scores of 750 out of 800 on the combined test generally correspond to the 99th percentile.

- 680 out of 800 corresponds to the 90th percentile.

GMAT Test Scores Distribution Snapshot - Total Score

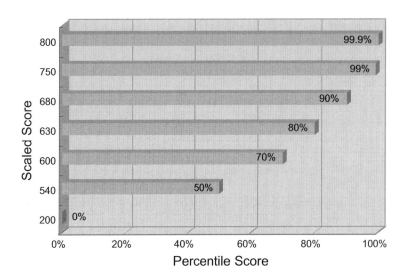

· Scaled scores of 750 out of 800 on the combined test generally correspond to the 99th percentile.

· 680 out of 800 corresponds to the 90th percentile

GMAT Test Scores Distribution Snapshot - AWA Score

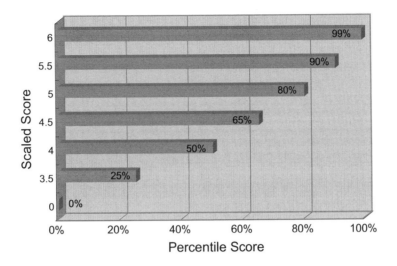

Since IR is relatively new, GMAC is yet to come up with 1 year data for percentile score vs. raw score distribution.

As stated earlier, one person and one computer programmed for grading (E-rater) score AWA based on essay content, organization, grammar and syntactic variety. E-rater is an electronic system that evaluates more than 50 structural and linguistic features. College and university faculty members trained as reviewers of the AWA essays consider the overall quality of your ideas, your overall ability to organize, develop, and express those ideas, the relevant supporting reasons and examples you cited, and your ability to write in standard written English. In considering the elements of standard written English, reviewers are trained to be sensitive and fair in evaluating the essays of non-native English speakers.

E-rater and independent readers agree, on average, 87 % to 94 % of the time. If the two ratings differ by more than one point, another evaluation by an expert reader is required to resolve the discrepancy and determine the final score.

AWA graders assign scores out of 6.0 based on intervals of 0.5 points. Your final, single score is an average of both the scores graded by E-rater and independent readers. AWA and IR scores are computed separately and have no bearings on any other GMAT scores.

Student Notes:

1.1.3 Overview of Basic GMAT Concepts

Various GMAT sections test students' understanding of fundamental quantitative concepts, and their knowledge, skills and analytical ability. To perform well on the test, students must master the basic underlying math and grammar principles and typical question types. The following is a quick overview.

Math Section

The Quantitative section measures your basic mathematical skills, understanding of elementary concepts, and the ability to reason quantitatively, solve quantitative problems, and interpret graphic data. Problem-Solving and Data-Sufficiency questions are intermingled throughout the section.

Basic Concepts:

- Integers and Prime numbers

- Fractions and Percentages

- Mark-up and Margin

- Exponents and Roots

- Equations and Inequalities

- Probability, Permutations and Combinations

- Statistics, Graph and Data Interpretation

- Coordinate Geometry, Area and Volume of Various Geometrical Objects

- Others to Be Discussed in Class

Basic Question Types:

- Solving Equations

- Profit, Cost and Break-Even Calculations

- Distance-Rate-Time Problems

- Divisibility

- Averages and Weighted Averages

- Word Problems

- Data and Graph Interpretation

- Area and Volume of Geometrical Shapes

- Mixture Problems

· Others to Be Discussed in Class

Verbal Section

The Verbal section of the GMAT measures your ability to:

· Correct written English to conform to standard grammar rules and styles

· Read, reason and evaluate arguments

· Speed read, comprehend and assess written English articles

Basic Grammar Rules:

· Subject-Verb Agreement

· Pronoun Reference

· Prepositions and Articles

· Verb Tenses and Voices

· Parallelism

· Idiomatic Usages

· Others to Be Discussed in Class

Basic Question Types:

· Sentence Correcton

· Reading Comprehension

· Critical Reasoning

· Please review the relevant sections for more details

Student Notes:

1.2   Key Test-taking and Preparation Strategies

The scores necessary to get into top schools are increasing year by year, making quality preparation an even greater necessity. Disciplined and dedicated preparation for the GMAT will allow you to get the best score possible on the exam and get into the school of your choice.

High quality preparation is essential to achieving your best score on the GMAT. High quality preparation means becoming intimately acquainted with the test structure, format, and the types of questions that are being asked. It means improving upon your weak areas through practice and repetition. It means developing your ability to answer correctly the tougher questions. It also means becoming aware of the types of answers that tend to be the correct ones.

Are there any advantages of taking a top-quality GMAT Prep course versus studying alone with the books, CDs , and online courses available in the market? It really depends on your academic background, study habits, availability and, ultimately, your desired test score. Preparing on your own can save you some financial resources, but may not be as effective as learning from instructors who dissect each answer and impart knowledge and advice from their own GMAT-taking and MBA experiences. Studies show that visualization and discussion in a seminar environment will enable you to recognize complex structures better than learning the same material in a non-interactive way.

In terms of general GMAT taking strategies, **we recommend**:

- Learn the most typical problems and answer types.

- Answer all questions.

- Guess and estimate when necessary.

- Try your best on the initial questions.

- Others to be discussed in class.

If you aim to achieve a top score, **we recommend**:

- Make a special effort to improve your weaknesses along with strengthening your expertise during practice.

- Locate or set up a serious test-taking environment in your house or a public library or a park or another facility so that you can exclusively focus on taking the mock tests.

- Download the free GMATPrep software from www.mba.com to practice official questions. It offers 90 questions (30-Quants; 45-Verbal; 15-IR).Save the two GMAT-Prep software tests for right before the actual test and practice the tests in a mock test setting of your choice so that your memory of the actual question types and difficulty levels which have appeared in prior GMAT tests stays fresh.

- Review all prior mistakes along with explanations.

- Make a list of those typical errors you tend to make and consciously remind yourself of them and refrain from making the same mistakes.

- Keep a light-hearted and positive attitude on the test day.

· Maintain strong momentum from beginning to end as the final problems can sometimes be equally as important as the initial ones.

Is it a good idea to reappear GMAT?

The answer is yes and No both. It depends on what was your score in the first attempt, and what is your current level of preparation. Reappearing GMAT more and more number of times does not mean that your score will improve. Approximate 25% candidates score lower that the score in the first attempt in the second sitting, while the average scaled score improves by average 33 point. In each successive attempt, your increment in scaled score diminishes.

So, the preparation and strategy to crack GMAT is utmost important!

Student Notes:

1.2.1 Problem Solving

The Problem Solving section of the GMAT tests your ability to solve questions and derive correct answers. Often these problems present you with an algebraic formula. It is important that you develop a good pace in your preparation for this section, as speed together with precision will help you do your best on the GMAT exam.
Main Strategies:

· First identify the underlying key mathematical concept of the problem.

· Determine the best way to approach the problem at hand. Common strategies include:

  – Applying algebraic and geometric formulae

  – Back solving

  – Approximation

  – Elimination

· Check your work and read the question again. You may have solved the problem correctly but simply failed to answer the question being asked.

· Take educated guesses when you see fit to do so.

· Others to be discussed in class.

Key test preparation principles include:

· Maintain speed and precision.

· Remember your Algebra and Geometry concepts.

· Review your Algebra and Geometry definitions.

Student Notes:

1.2.2 Data Sufficiency

Data-Sufficiency questions are designed to measure your ability to:

· Analyze a quantitative problem

· Recognize relevant information

· Determine whether there is sufficient information to solve a problem

Data-Sufficiency questions are accompanied by some initial information and two statements, labeled (1) and (2). You must decide whether the statements given offer enough data to enable you to answer the question. Data Sufficiency questions do not ask for actual number solutions, and instead they ask simply: Is the information given adequate to solve a question?

Two statements are laid out as two possible conditions. It is important to analyze each statement independently from the other statement. In other words, you cannot mix the information from one statement with the other.

There are two common types of Data Sufficiency questions:

· Close-ended: Is "Y" divisible by 3?

· Open-ended: What is the value of "X"?

There are five answer choices for Data Sufficiency.

A: Statement (1) is sufficient and (2) is insufficient.

B: Statement (1) is insufficient and (2) is sufficient.

C: A combination of both statements is sufficient. Either statement alone is insufficient.

D: Both statements are sufficient independently.

E: Neither the combination nor either individual statement is sufficient.

In a close-ended question, you can judge whether each statement is sufficient by determining if its answer is always Yes or always No. A statement is insufficient if its answer is sometimes Yes or sometimes No.

In an open-ended question, you can judge whether each statement is sufficient by determining if its answer results in a single value. A statement is insufficient if its answer leads to a range of values, instead of a specific value.

Other strategies include:

· Memorize the standardized answer choices for Data Sufficiency questions.

· Evaluate each statement or equation individually and then together.

· Others to be discussed in class.

Student Notes:

1.2.3 Sentence Correction

The Sentence Correction section tests your knowledge of written English grammar by asking you which of the five choices best expresses an idea or relationship. This section gives you a sentence that may or may not contain errors of grammar or usage. You must select either the answer that best corrects the sentence or the answer stating that the sentence is correct as is. The questions will require you to be familiar with the stylistic conventions and grammatical rules of standard written English and to demonstrate your ability to improve incorrect or ineffective expressions.

This section tests two broad aspects of language proficiency:

· Correct expression

· Effective expression

A correct sentence is grammatically correct and structurally sound. It conforms to all the rules of standard written English such as subject-verb agreement, verb tense consistency, modifier reference and position, idiomatic expressions and parallel construction.

In addition to being correct, a sentence needs to be effective. It should express an idea or relationship clearly and concisely, as well as grammatically. A best choice should have no superfluous words or unnecessarily complicated expressions. This does not mean that the shortest choice is always the best answer. Proper diction is another important part of effectiveness. It refers to the standard dictionary meanings of words and the appropriateness of words in context. In evaluating the diction of a sentence, you must be able to recognize whether the words are well chosen, accurate, and suitable for the context.

One common error that test takers often make in the Sentence Correction section is choosing an answer that sounds good. Do not go on with your gut feeling in this section. Remember your grammar and look for errors in construction (e.g., noun-verb agreement) and eliminate answers that you are sure are incorrect.

Follow the procedure given below.

· Look over answer choices and note for clearly identifiable patterns.

· Focus your attention on the most crucial grammatical issue in the problem.

· Look for patterns in the first and last word(s) across all answer choices, as those parts of the sentence often demonstrate major grammatical differences.

· Look over each answer choice, as you can eliminate the wrong answer by focusing on not only the grammatical difference from other choices, but also the answer's own language style, word usage and idiomatic expressions.

· Keep in mind also that the GMAT prefers active to passive constructions.

· Eliminate clearly incorrect answers.

· Select the answer which is grammatically correct, idiomatically acceptable and the most effective.

· Others to be discussed in class.

Student Notes:

1.2.4 Critical Reasoning

The Critical Reasoning section tests your ability to make arguments, evaluate arguments, and formulate or evaluate a plan of action. In this section we recommend that you read the questions carefully and identify the assumption implicit in the statement with a heightened awareness of any weakness in the argument.
Please bear in mind the following when you practice in this section:

- Break the argument down into its parts: conclusion, evidence and assumption.

- The main argument types include:

  - Cause and Effect

  - Comparison/Analogy

  - Representative Sample

  - Number and Logic Based

  - Implementation

- Be familiar with major critical reasoning questions category:

  (1) **a) Assumption Questions**

  - **Assumption**
  - **Weakening**
  - **Strengthening**
  - **Flaw**

  (2) **b) Inference/Conclusion Questions**

  (3) **c) Paradox/Explain Questions**

  (4) **d) Method of Reasoning Questions**

- Determine how the question fits into these types.

- Eliminate clearly incorrect answers when they are totally irrelevant or the opposite of the desired answer.

- Others to be discussed in class.

Student Notes:

1.2.5 Reading Comprehension

You may see as many as 4 passages in the Reading Comprehension section up to 350 words in each passage, followed by 3 or 4 interpretive, applied, and inferential questions. The topics are typically related to social sciences such as politics and history, physical or biological sciences such as geology and astronomy, business-related areas such as marketing, economics and human resource management, along with other advanced subjects.

Because the Reading Comprehension section includes passages from various different content areas, you may have general knowledge about some of the topics. However, no specific familiarity of the material is required. All questions are to be answered on the basis of what is stated or implied in the reading material.

Reading Comprehension questions measure your ability to speed read, understand, analyze, and apply information and concepts presented in written English. It evaluates your ability to:

- Understand words, terms and statements.

- Understand the ideas, concepts and logical relationships between significant perspectives and to evaluate the importance of arguments.

- Draw inferences from facts and statements.

- Understand and follow the development of quantitative concepts as presented. Then interpret and use the data to reach conclusions.

We recommend the following general guidelines:

- Quickly scan the passage to understand the underlying theme. Read the first and last sentence particularly carefully.

- Read the passage in detail. Note its main structure.

- Pay special attention to the usage of transitional words that change the passage's flow, such as yet, though, however, despite, etc. These transitional words often highlight important information in the passage.

- Note different perspectives presented and the relationship amongst them.

- Quickly scan through the questions and answers to develop a general sense of the focus of the question.

- Read the answers to note the possibilities addressed. At this point eliminate any clearly wrong answers.

- Others to be discussed in class.

Student Notes:

1.2.6 Analytical Writing Assessment

The first section you will encounter on the GMAT is the Analytical Writing Assessment (AWA). The AWA requires you to write one essay on 'analysis of an argument' in 30 minutes. The argument that you will find on the test concern topic of general interest related to business or a variety of other subjects.

The AWA section receives a score from 0-6, in increments of 0.5.

- 0 indicates incomprehensibility.

- 6 indicates a well-focused and clear essay.

The AWA score is not reflected in the combined verbal and quantitative overall score, but is still an important aspect of your MBA application and should not be neglected. By focusing on clarity and precision rather than on saying something complicated or brilliant, you will score higher on this portion of the GMAT.

The AWA section is designed to directly measure your ability to think critically through the complexities of an issue and to communicate your ideas through substantiated reasoning. The Analysis of an Argument tests your ability to formulate an appropriate and constructive critique of a specific conclusion based on a rigorous approach. You will need to analyze the supporting logic behind a given argument and write a critique of that argument. Remember your task is to examine and critique the given argument, not to present your own views on the subject.

Consider the following when developing your essay:

- The underlying debatable assumptions behind the argument.

- The alternative explanations or counter-examples might weaken the conclusion.

- The type of evidence could help strengthen or refute the argument.

For the AWA section, we recommend that you make a consistent effort to:

- Brush up on your typing skills.

- Be careful not to make careless mistakes in spelling or grammar.

- Make the reader aware of your essay structure.

- Others to be discussed in class.

Student Notes:

1.2.7 Integrated Reasoning

IR sub-section will follow AWA task. This is what GMAC states about IR. The Integrated Reasoning measures your ability to comprehend and evaluate multiple types of information—textual, tabular, graphic, visual, quantitative, and verbal; it applies quants and verbal reasoning to solve problems in relation to one another.

The Integrated Reasoning section differs from the Quantitative and Verbal sections in two ways:

- IR comprises both quantitative and verbal reasoning, either discretely or blended, and

- IR prompts use four different response formats rather than only traditional multiple-choice format used for quantitative and verbal questions.

Four types of questions are used in the Integrated Reasoning section are:

- Table Analysis

- Graphics Interpretation

- Two-Part Analysis

- Multi-Source Reasoning

In a nut shell, the IR questions assess your ability to apply, infer, evaluate, recognize, and strategize information from multiple sources.

- Apply questions

    Apply questions measure your ability to comprehend the concepts in the information given and apply them to a new situation.

- Evaluate, and Inference questions

    Evaluate questions measure your ability to make decisions based on the quality of information. These questions are very similar to Critical Reasoning questions, in which you are asked the questions on Strengthen/Weaken the argument, Sufficiency of the information to make a decision- some aspect of Data Sufficiency, Inference and Flaw in reasoning.

- Recognize questions

    Recognize questions measure your ability to identify the information that includes some facts or aspects and their relationships. You may be asked to recognize agreement and disagreement in the information given, strength of correlation between two variables, compare two or more data points, observe data and deduce information.

- Strategic questions

  Strategize questions tests your ability on how you gain an objective within the constraints. You may be asked to select a course of action that gives desired results, and optimise resources.

Student Notes:

1.2.8   Test Preparation Advice

During your GMAT preparation, be sure to incorporate the following study skills:

- Apply a systematic approach to your test. Take all questions seriously and answer them. Leaving questions unanswered is not helpful on the GMAT CAT.

- Create a study environment that is as similar as possible to the actual test setting, which typically includes a quiet space, possibly a computer room or an office environment.

- Do take two breaks during a practice test of approximately 5 minutes each. In the actual test center, you will be allowed to take two breaks of maximum 8 minutes each during sections. However, the break is limited to taking some drinks, and snack that you bring with you.

- Eliminate distractions and be conscious of time. Especially when you are taking practice tests, be as aware of the clock as you will need to be on the actual exam.

- After completing a practice test, be sure to go over the questions you answered incorrectly. This is the only way to improve. You must understand your mistakes so that you will not make them on the test.

- AND practice, practice, practice!

Remember that the actual exam is on the computer so take advantage of opportunities to practice with Computer Adaptive Tests. For many test-takers, reading large amounts of material on the screen is not easy. It not only dries out their eyes but also makes it hard to absorb the material. Simply practice reading etc. on the computer. The only way to improve is to practice.

Student Notes:

1.3 Taking the GMAT

1.3.1 Schedule Your Test

When setting a test date, look up test centers at http://www.mba.com/the-gmat.aspx. Keep in mind the following:

- Consider the times of day you tend to be able to concentrate best. Take your test in the morning or afternoon accordingly.

- Make sure the week before your test day will not be a stressful one. This will help you concentrate, be well rested, calm and in the right frame of mind to ace the GMAT.

- Be aware of application deadlines and do your best to provide yourself with enough time after the exam to focus on the other parts of your Business School applications.

Remember to select:

- · The best possible time of day for you.

- · A low stress week.

- · AND give yourself sufficient time to prepare fully for the test.

In the final week before your test, remember:

- · Don't cram.

- · Take a practice test(s). You can often even do this at the test center (a good way to ensure that you will not get lost on the day of the test). Again don't cram.

- · Get solid rest.

1.3.2 Test Fee

The fee to take the GMAT is U.S. $250 worldwide. The fee for rescheduling the date, time, or location of the test is U.S. $50 for each appointment you change.

Should you want to reschedule the GMAT, avoid the forfeiture of your test fee by allowing at least 7 calendar days between the day you reschedule your appointment and your test day. Appointments cannot be rescheduled for a date that is more than one year after the original appointment date.

If you cancel the test appointment, a partial refund of U.S. $80 will be given if it is canceled at least 7 calendar days before your original test day.

The rescheduling fee and cancellation refund amount are subject to change without notice

1.3.3 On the Test Day

Here is a summary of to-do items for the test day:

· Bring all necessary documents such as identification cards (IDs), the registration ticket and the names of the schools to which you would like send your test score. (Bring two forms of ID in case one has expired or is not acceptable to the test center.)

· Bring something warm to put on in case the room is too cold. According to test center rules, you have to wear the sweater or coat rather than put it around your shoulders. So make sure that the additional layer of sweater or coat is comfortable in a test-taking setting.

· Also be sure you can remove a layer of clothing in case the room is hot.

· Bring something light to drink or eat. A bottle of water or a soft drink with a cap is preferred over a can so that you can minimize the chances of spilling. (Though you can not take anything into the testing room, you will be assigned a small locker. During your 8-minute breaks, you can have a few sips to stay hydrated or a bite to eat if you get hungry. Normally test centers allow you to put it outside on a desk or at an easily reachable spot or inside your locker so that you can quickly grab the drink or the food.)

· No testing aids such as study notes, calculators, cellphones and PDAs are allowed. Normally one note-board or booklet will be provided.

At the test:

· Follow your normal routine.

· Arrive at the test at least 30 minutes early.

· Do concentrate on all questions. A myth that first 10 questions are more important is wrong. At the beginning of each section, the total number of questions and the total time allowed are stated.

· Maintain a focused mind and a positive winning attitude throughout the entire test.

· Do not panic. Focus on one question at a time. Focus on one section at a time. Do not think beyond your current section and lose your concentration.

- Do not get fixated and spend unreasonable time on any single question. It will not make or break your score. Because the score per section is partially based on the number of questions you answer, try to answer as many questions as you can.

- Do not leave any questions unanswered before the section time runs out. Always submit an answer after some educated or blind guesses. Remember that you cannot skip questions or change an answer once you confirm it.

- If a few questions or passages are difficult to understand, do not let that prompt you to cancel your score entirely. You can never know.

- If something is wrong with the computer, or if someone is bothering you, or if its miserably hot etc., signal to the exam proctor. The proctor observes the examination area all the time.

- Pace yourself and keep track of your progress by checking the amount of time you have left on the test screen. The first section is of 60 minutes and other two sections are 75 minutes each. You have about 2.5 minutes per IR question, about 2 minutes per Quantitative question, and about 1.75 minutes per Verbal question.

- Pay attention to the number of questions that remain in a section. There are 37 quantitative section questions. There are 41 verbal section questions.

- Clicking on "HELP" or hiding the "TIME" information doesnt pause or stop the time.

- Between test sections, replenish your supply of note-board paper. Take advantage of breaks. Rest your eyes, as the computer screen is difficult to stare at for 4 hours straight.

Student Notes:

1.3.4 Score Report

Your Total score and Quantitative and Verbal section scores are available upon your completion of the test. The only opportunity that you will have to cancel your scores is immediately after you complete the test, but before you view your scores. A message will ask you if you want to cancel your scores; you will be given two minute time to either 'Accept' or 'Reject' the score.. You cannot cancel your scores after they are displayed or reported to you.

If you cancel your scores, they cannot be reinstated later. A score cancellation notice will be sent to you and your selected schools. It will remain a part of your permanent record and will be reported on all of your future score reports. The test will not be refunded and will be accounted for as one taken test.

The official score report is available online. Through a direct e-mail 20 days after the test, you will be notified of the accessibility of your online official score report, which is also available to the schools you selected as recipients. Official Score Reports are now mailed to the student by request only.

Official GMAT score reports, which include the AWA score, will be mailed to you and your designated score report recipients (schools) approximately two weeks after the test. You must respond to both essays and each multiple-choice section of the test to get an official score report.

During the test, if you click "Section Exit" or "Test Quit," you will have to confirm your choice. If you clicked it by mistake or change your mind, just select the option "Return to Where I Was." Once you exit a section or quit a test, you won't be able to return to it and you won't receive a score for any section, regardless how many questions you have answered.

You may take the GMAT only once every 31 days and no more than five times within any 12-month period. The retest policy applies even if you cancel your score or quit a test within that time period. Official GMAT score results are kept on file for 10 years. All your scores and cancellations within the last five years will be reported to the institutions you designate as score recipients.

On your test day before you take the test, you may select up to five schools to receive your scores. Once you have made your selection, you will not be able to change or delete the list of schools. If you would like to send your scores to more schools, you may order additional score reports at a cost of U.S. $28 per school.

You may request that your essays be rescored if you have reason to believe that your AWA scores are not accurate. The multiple-choice quantitative and verbal sections of the test cannot be rescored. Independent readers will rescore your essay for a fee of U.S. $45.

Requests for rescoring must be made within six months of your test date. Rescoring may result in increases or decreases in your original AWA score. The rescoring results are final. Revised results will be sent to you and the schools you designated as score recipients within three weeks of your request.

Student Notes:

Chapter 2

Grammar Review

2.1 Noun

Nouns are used as subjects of sentences and as the objects of verbs and prepositions.

2.1.1 Common and Proper Nouns

Generally there are two types of nouns - common nouns and proper nouns.

- Common nouns refer to any place, person or thing, for example, girl, apartment, city.

- Proper nouns refer to particular places, persons and things, for example, Mark, New York, the White House.

2.1.2 Singular and Plural Nouns

Nouns can also be categorized as singular nouns and plural nouns. Sometimes certain nouns are used exclusively as either singular or plural nouns. That means they do not have a corresponding word to their own singular or plural form.

- Singular nouns are used for single occurrence, single person, single item, and etc.

- Plural nouns are used for more than more occurrences, persons, items, and etc.

A quick comparison table of some tricky nouns in their singular and plural forms:

Alumnus	Alumni
Bacterium	Bacteria
Criterion	Criteria
Formula	Formulae
Medium	Media
Phenomenon	Phenomena

There are some singular nouns often mistaken as plural nouns because they end with "s".

Citrus

Economics

Glasses

Means

Measles

News

Physics

Scissors

Series

Species

Statistics

2.1.3   Countable and Uncountable Nouns

Another way to group nouns is separating them into countable nouns and non-countable nouns. Countable nouns usually have both singular and plural forms. Uncountable nouns are used just as singular.

· Countable nouns can be counted in the number of 1, 2, 3…Examples are desk, pen, person.

· Uncountable nouns can not be counted in any numbers. Rather, they are considered an entire item. Some most commonly used uncountable nouns are water, health, and money.

Other examples of uncountable nouns include:

Advice

Anger

Baggage

Beauty

Gasoline

Information

Luggage

Smog

Wheat

Sometimes a noun is used as an uncountable noun when it is referred to the entire idea or substance, but it can be used as a countable noun when used in a context involving:

⟹   Countable pieces or containers for things.

Uncountable: I prefer tea to coke.
Countable: Two teas (two cups of tea) for us, please.

⟹   Different brands, makes, or types.

Uncountable: I love cheese.
Countable: There are so many cheeses to choose from.

⟹   A specific example.

Uncountable: She has shiny hair.
Countable: I found a hair today in my sandwich. It grossed me out.

Uncountable: He is great at sport.
Countable: Skiing is a popular sport in Austria.

2.1.4 Collective Nouns

Certain nouns are used to just describe a collection of people, items, or events in their entirety. Even though they are referring to more than one thing in the collection, they are singular. However, when they are used to represent a number of collections, then they are plural.
Examples include:

Audience

Business

Choir

Committee

Company

Crowd

Family

Flock

Government

Group

Majority

Nation

Pack

Team

The Public

Unit

2.2 Pronoun

2.2.1 Pronoun Types

A pronoun is a part of speech that is typically used as a substitute for a noun or noun phrase. There are **eight subclasses** of pronouns, although some forms belong to more than one group:

(1) **personal pronouns** (I, you, he/she/it, we, you, they)

  · Make sure sentences use them consistently

(2) **possessive pronouns** (my/mine, his/her/its/hers, their/theirs, our/ours, etc.)

  · Do not change the gender of noun as in French

(3) **reflexive pronouns** (myself, yourself, him/herself, ourselves, themselves, etc.)

  · No reflexive verbs in English

(4) **demonstrative pronouns** (this/these, that/those)

  · Nearness in location
  · That (pronoun) vs. That (conjunction)

(5) **reciprocal pronouns** (each other, one another)

(6) **interrogative pronouns** (who, what, when, where, why etc.)

  · Five w's of a journalist's first paragraph

(7) **relative pronouns** (who, that, what, which etc.)

  · Related different clauses in a sentence to each other
  · That vs. Which: restrictive vs. non-restrictive clause
  · Who vs. Whom: take subject vs. take object (Please see explanation later.)

(8) **indefinite pronouns** (any, none, somebody, nobody, anyone, etc.)

  · none = singular (when it means "not one"); all = plural (if countable);
  · much = can't be counted; many = can be counted
  · less = can't be counted; fewer = can be counted

2.2.2 Nominative and Objective Cases

There are two pronominal cases: nominative (subject) and objective (object).

Subject: I, you, he/she/it, we, you, they.

Object: me, you, him/her/it, us, you, them.

Notice that the second person (both singular and plural) has only one form, *you*. The object case is used after verbs and prepositions:

We met *her* in a bookstore. She went to school with *us*.

Be careful of objects that consist of a proper noun (name) + a pronoun:

The puppy looked across the table at *Sarah* and *me*.

These situations can seem confusing, but there is an easy method to tell which pronoun (nominative or objective) is required. Just remove the noun from the sentence to see if it still makes sense. If it does (as in "The puppy looked across the table at me"), then you have selected the correct pronoun. If it does not (as in "The puppy looked across the table at I"), then you should go back and check whether you selected the correct case for the pronoun (in this case it is the object of a preposition, *at*, so it should be in the objective case).

The relative pronoun *who* also has an objective case form, *whom*:

I kicked the girl *who* tried to steal my coat.

(I kicked the girl. *She* tried to steal my coat.)

I smiled at the girl *whom* I had kicked.

(I smiled at the girl. I had kicked *her*.)

2.2.3 Possessive Forms

All these pronouns have possessive forms that **do not** have apostrophes:

my, your, his/her/its, our, your, their

These act as adjectives, and are followed by nouns. If there is no noun and the possessive form is used by itself, this form is said to be disjunctive:

mine, yours, his/hers/its, ours, yours, theirs.

Again, there is no apostrophe. The relative pronoun *who* has the possessive form *whose*:

I comforted the dog *whose* tail had been stepped on.

One is used as a supplementary pronoun; it **does** have an apostrophe in the possessive:

One can only do *one's* best.

Note that *one's* is used only if the subject *one* is present; following with *his* would not be acceptable.

2.2.4 Agreement & Reference

There are several pronominal forms which seem to be plural but act as singular, taking singular verbs and singular pronouns if they act as antecedents. The most common of these words are *another, any, anybody, anything, each, either, every, everybody, neither, no one, nobody, none (not one)*, etc.; they must be followed by a singular verb, whatever the meaning might indicate:

> *Not one* of the bananas *was* ripe.

> *Everybody* wanted *his or her* own way.

Always look back to see what the pronoun refers to; where there is a generalization, it is sometimes tempting to treat a singular as a plural:

> *Man*, in all *his* glory, has ascended to the top of the food chain.

2.3 Adjective

2.3.1 Usage

An adjective is a descriptive word which qualifies a noun, making it more specific:

> The *red* car.

> The *old red* car.

> The *big old red* car.

> The two *young* professors lived in Greewich Village.

> A *bright* light flashed through the window of the house.

Adjectives are usually arranged in the order of specificity. Words normally used to perform other grammatical functions may be used as adjectives. These can be recognized by their position before the noun to which they apply:

> *remote-control* car

> *war* effort

> *Christmas* cookies

> *spring* carnival

Adjectives can also be used to form a **predicate** with the verb to *be*:

> Chocolate *is yummy*.

Normally, only "true" adjectives can be used to form this kind of predicate. It is not possible to say:

> **Wrong:** The cookies were *Christmas*, or

> **Wrong:** The carnival was *spring*.

In such cases, it is necessary to use the prop-word, *one*:

The cookies were *Christmas ones.*

There are three forms of a "true" adjective.

Normal:	big	beautiful
Comparative:	bigger	more beautiful
Superlative:	biggest	most beautiful

No agreement to noun is necessary for an adjective.

Student Notes:

2.4 Adverb

An adverb is a part of speech used mainly to modify verbs but also adjectives and other adverbs. Adverbs describe how, where or when.

2.4.1 Adverbial Forms

Adverbs are formed in a few different ways:

Most adverbs are formed from adjectives by the addition of the ending *"-ly"* (as in suddenly, playfully, interestingly) or *"-ally"* after words in *-ic* (as in, automatically).

Some adverbs are formed from nouns in combination with other suffixes: *-wise* (as in, clockwise, lengthwise) and *-ward(s)* (as in, northward, westward, skyward).

Some common adverbs have **no** suffixes, as in: *here/there, now, well, just.*

Some adverbs can qualify other adverbs (the most common are intensifiers, such as very, as in "very quick").

Some adverbs have the **same** form as their adjective counterpart, e.g., *fast, long, first.*

Not all words ending in -ly are adverbs: *lovely, ungainly*, and *likely* are adjectives. The word *only* and *early* may be either.

2.4.2 Adverbial Positions

Adverbs modify verbs in the same way adjectives qualify nouns.

The adverb **often follows the verb** it modifies:

> I shouted *loudly* to my friends across the theater.

Sometimes it precedes the verb:

> I *really* wanted to talk to her.

Sometimes position determines meaning:

> I think *clearly*. (My thinking is clear.)

> I *clearly* think. (It is clear that I think.)

Where emphasis is needed, the adverb may be put first, and the verb and subject inverted:

> *Never* have I seen such an ugly dog.

Student Notes:

2.5 Adverb vs. Adjective

2.5.1 Position and Meaning

When adverbs are used to modify adjectives, it is important to work out the relationships between them:

> She heard an *odd*, chilling sound.

> She heard an *oddly* chilling sound.

If one is not careful it is easy to confuse whether a word is an adverb or an adjective, and in either case, which other word it is modifying in the sentence.

The change from adjective to adverb can change the meaning drastically:

> The centaur appeared *quick*.

> The centaur appeared *quickly*.

In this example when the adjective is used, it appears that the centaur is quick, whereas when the adverb is used, it is the centaur's appearance which occurred quickly.

Good vs. well: Both *good* and *well* can be used as adjectives. When used as adjectives, *good* refers to morality or quality and *well* refers to health. However, only *well* can be used as adverb and *good* is always an adjective.

Correct:

> I feel *good* about my work.

> I feel *well*.

> I am *well*.

> I'm doing *well*.

Wrong: I am doing *good*.

2.5.2 Adverb and Adjective

Great care must be taken to align only with the word it actually modifies, because its positioning can affect the meaning of the sentence:

> I ate some peas *only* yesterday - I don't need to eat any today.

> I *only* ate some peas yesterday - I didn't do anything else.

> I ate *only* some peas yesterday - I didn't eat anything else.

> *Only* I ate some peas yesterday - nobody else had any.

Early may be both adjective and adverb:

> I take the *early* train.

> I get up *early* to take the train.

2.5.3 Adjective Only

Notice that some verbs may take adjectives to complete the meaning required (complementary adjectives). These verbs cannot form a complete thought without the required adjectives:

> He looks *confused* today.

> The music seemed *loud.*

Likely
Special care must be taken with the adjective **likely**. It is often mistaken for an adverb because of its form, but this is not an acceptable usage, for example:

> **Correct**: The Republic is *likely* to fall.

> **Wrong**: The Republic will likely fall.

Like (used as adjective or preposition)
Like, with its opposite *unlike*, should be treated as an adjective or a preposition; that is, it must always have a noun to relate to. A predicate is formed with the verb *to be*:

> Life is *like* a box of chocolates. (Life resembles a box of chocolates.)

Used in the form of a phrase, *like* will link two nouns (or noun phrases) of the same kind. In this case, *like* functions as a preposition, a phrase-maker, and it is categorized so in some grammar books.

> *Like* any politician, he often told half-truths.

Like vs. Such As
In the above example, *like* is used to introduce similarity between two items or persons. This is an accepted usage in Sentence Correction on the GMAT. In other words, *like* cannot be used to introduce examples or a subset of a category, which should be used following *such as*.

> **Correct**: I enjoy playing musical instruments *such as* piano and violin.

> **Wrong**: I enjoy playing musical instruments *like* piano and violin.

In sum, on the GMAT, use *like* before a noun or pronoun when emphasizing similar characteristics between two persons, groups or things. Use **such as** before a noun or phrase when introducing examples.

Like vs. As/As If/As though
Use *like* before a noun or pronoun. Use *as* before a clause, adverb or prepositional phrase. Use *as if* and *as though* before a clause. *Like* is generally used as a preposition in such a context. *As* is generally used as an adverb while sometimes serving as a preposition with the meaning of "in the capacity of." As you can tell, the focus of the comparison shifts from the noun when used with like to the verb when used with *as*, *as if*, or *as though.*

> My mother's cheesecake tastes *like glue.*

> I love frozen pizza because there is no other snack *like* it.

> My mother's cheesecake tastes great, *as* a mother's cheesecake should.

> There are times, *as* now, that learning grammar becomes important.

He golfed well again, *as* in the tournament last year.

He served *as* captain in the navy.

He often told half-truths, *as* any politician would.

He looks ***as if*** he knows me.

It looked ***as if*** a storm were on the way.

He yelled at me *as though* it were my fault.

The same rule applies when you use the expressions *seem like* and *look like*.

Correct:

He *seemed like* a nice guy at first.

That *looks like* a very tasty cake.

Wrong: It *seemed* like he liked me.

Correct: It *seemed as if* he liked me.

Here the comparison is with a clause, not a noun.

Due to

Due to is also used adjectivally, and must have a noun to attach itself to:

My failure, *due to* a long-term illness during the semester, was disappointing.
(That is, the failure was attributable to the long-term illness, not the disappointment, which would have had other causes, such as the failure.)

Owing to

If an adverbial link is needed, the expression *owing to* has lost its exclusively adjectival quality:

My failure was disappointing *owing to* a long-term illness during the semester.
(In this case, the disappointment at the failure was caused by the long-term illness during the semester.)

2.6 Preposition

Prepositions are words that are placed before a noun making a particular relationship between it and the word to which it is attached.

2.6.1 Preposition Types

There are a few types of prepositions:

1) **simple prepositions**: these are the most common prepositions, such as: *in, on, of, at, from, among, between, over, with, through, without.*

2) **compound prepositions**: two prepositions used together as one, such as: *into, onto/on to (on to is British English, onto is American English), out of.*

3) **complex prepositions**: a two- or three-word phrase that functions in the same way as a simple preposition, as in: *according to, as well as, except for, in favor of.*

Preposition i.e. pre position. Prepositions always occur before the thing they refer to.
In: I was born *in* that house. (Here that house is the object of the preposition *in*)
Prepositional phrases may be adjectival or adverbial, according to what they modify:

> The girl *in my science class* kissed me.

Here, *in my science class* qualifies *girl*, and it is adjectival, but in

> The girl kissed me *in my science class.*

in my science class modifies *kissed*, indicating where the kiss took place, and it is therefore adverbial.
Between refers to two things only; for more than two, use *among*.

> I sat *between* two very large people.

> We split the loot *among* the four of us.

2.6.2 Prepositions Frequently Misused

You should use prepositions carefully. Some prepositions are used interchangeably and carelessly.
For example:
beside vs. *besides*

> *beside* - at the side of someone or something

> Frank stood *beside* Henry.

> *besides* - in addition to

> *Besides* his Swiss bank account he has many others in Austria.

Exception: some idioms do not refer directly to either direct meaning.

> She was beside herself with emotion.

The use of 'of' Phrases such as: could of, must of are **incorrect** forms for could have, must have etc.
between vs. *among*
Use the preposition *among* in situations involving more than two persons or things and use *between* in situations involving only two persons or things.

> The money was divided *among* the workers.

> The money was divided *between* the two boxers.

at vs. *with*: usually at a thing but with a person. Exceptions include throw something *at* somebody *with* something, be angry *at* someone, be pleased *with* something, and others.
For example,

> I went at Roger *with* a bat.

What's wrong with this sentence? Nothing actually, it is grammatically correct. It is simply an odd usage of the prepositions.
Be careful to use the right preposition for the meaning you want; *agree with* differs in meaning from *agree to, compare with* is distinct from *compare to*, and so on.

The expressions *superior to, preferable to* and *different from* are the only standard forms.
Student Notes:

2.6.3 Idioms with Prepositions

A

a sequence **of**

in accordance **with**

be accused **of**

acquiesce **in**

access **to**

adhere **to**, *be an adherent* **of** *(follower)*

affinity **with**

be afraid **of**

agree **with** *(a person/idea)*

agree **to** *(a proposal or action)*

aim **at**

allow **for**

an instance **of**

analogy **with**, *analogous* **to**

be attended **by** *(not with)*

attend **to**

appeal **to** *(a person)*

approval **of**

as a result **of**

associate **with**

attribute A **to** *B (B is attributed to A)*

authority **on** B

be based **on**

have belief **in**

be capable **of**

*be careful **of***

<u>*C*</u>

*be capable **of***

*care **about** – be considerate of; to think about*

*care **for** - like*

*center **on**, center **upon** (not round)*

*collide **with** (not against)*

*comment **on***

*compare **with**, in comparison **with** (used when emphasizing differences)*

*compare **to** (used when emphasizing similarities)*

*comply **with***

*be composed **by** – be created by*

*be composed **of** – to be made up of*

*comprise **of***

*be concerned **with***

*concur **in** (an opinion)*

*concur **with** (a person)*

*conducive **to***

*conform **to***

in** conformity **with

*consist **of***

in** contrast **to

*contrast A **with** B*

*credit **with** (not to)*

*give someone credit **for** (something or doing something)*

<u>*D*</u>

in** danger **of

*debate **on**, debate **over***

*decide **on***

*depend **on** (whether..., not if...), be dependent **on**, be independent **from***

*determine **by***

*differ **from** - to be unlike something; to be different from*

*differ **with** - to disagree with someone*

*discourage **from***

*feel disgusted **with** (not at)*

---

at one's disposal

distinguish *from*

be drawn *to*

<u>E</u>

be embarrassed *by* (not at)

end *with*, end *in* (not by)

be envious *of*, jealous *of*

be equal *to* (not as)

be essential *to*

except *for*, except that...

<u>F</u>

be familiar *with*

be fascinated *by*

<u>H</u>

be hindered *by*

<u>I</u>

be identical *with*, be identical *to*

be independent *from*

be indifferent *towards*

inherit *from*

instill something *in* someone (not instill someone with)

invest *in*

involve *in* (not by)

insist *on*, insist that someone do something

be isolated *from*

<u>J</u>

judge *by* (not on)

<u>M</u>

mistake *for*

<u>N</u>

native *to*

a native *of*

necessity *of*, necessity *for*

a need *for*

<u>O</u>

*be oblivious **of**, oblivious **to***

P

*participate **in***

*preferable **to***

*prevent **from***

*profit **by** (not from)*

*prohibit **from***

*protest **against** (not at)*

R

*receptive **of**, receptive **to***

*be related **to***

*relations **with** (not towards)*

*repent **of***

*in response **to***

*result **from***

*result **in***

S

*be in search **of** (not for)*

*be sensible **of***

*be sensitive **to***

*separate **from** (not away from or out)*

*similar **to***

*be sparing **of** (not with)*

*be solicitous **of** (not to)*

*suffer **from** (not with)*

*be superior **to***

*subscribe **to***

*sacrifice **for***

T

*tendency **to** (not for)*

*tinker **with** (not at, although this is British English usage)*

*be tolerant **of** (not to)*

W

*wait **for** - to spend time in waiting for someone or something*

*wait **on** – to serve someone, typically used in a restaurant setting*

2.7 Verb

A class of words that serve to indicate the occurrence or performance of an action, or the existence of a state or condition. English verbs are normally expressed in the infinitive form, together with "to". For example, to run, to walk, to work, etc.

2.7.1 Transitive and Intransitive Verbs

A verb is said to be **transitive** if it needs an object to complete the meaning:

> Joern *kicked his brother.*

It is **intransitive** if the meaning is complete in itself:

> I *smiled.*

> The rain *falls.*

Some verbs may be either transitive or intransitive (meaning that they do not require an object to be complete, but they can take one to add detail):

> I *ate.*

> I *ate pudding.*

2.7.2 Active and Passive Voices

Transitive verbs may appear in **active** or **passive** constructions. In active verb constructions, the subject is directly concerned with the verbal process; it is the agent:

> The hit-man *killed* my boyfriend.

When an active construction is made passive, the object becomes the subject, and the relationship is reversed, so that the subject is now acted upon, 'passive':

> My boyfriend *was killed* by the hit-man.

2.7.3 Major Tenses

You will not have to memorize all of the commonly used tenses for the GMAT, but a quick review of the tenses and their respective meanings will help you make sense of what can be a confusing topic.

Tense	Example
Simple Present (action frequently happening in the present)	**He laughs.** **They laugh.**
Perfect Progressive (action ongoing at this moment)	He is laughing. They are laughing.
Present Perfect (action started previously and completed thus far)	**He has laughed.** **They have laughed.**
Simple Past (completed action)	**He laughed.** **They laughed.**
Present Perfect Progressive (action started previously and ongoing at this moment)	He has been laughing. They have been laughing.
Past Perfect (action completed before another past time)	**He had laughed.** **They had laughed.**
Future (action to occur later)	**He will laugh.** **They will laugh.**
Future Progressive (action ongoing at a later time)	He will be laughing. They will be laughing.
Future Perfect (action regarded as completed at a later time)	**He will have laughed.** **They will have laughed.**
Future Perfect Progressive (action started at a later time and ongoing)	He will have been laughing. They will have been laughing.

Verbal Tense Examples:

Present: ring

Past: rang

Past Participle: rung

Present: walk

Past: walked

Past Participle: walked

More examples:

Past: danced

Present: dance

Future: will dance

Past perfect: had danced

Present perfect: have danced

Future perfect: will have danced

Present Progressive: am dancing

Conditional: would dance

Common Irregular Verbs

Infinitive Participle	Part Participle	Future Participle
do	did	done
go	went	gone
take	took	taken
rise	rose	risen
begin	began	begun
swim	swam	swum
throw	threw	thrown
break	broke	broken
burst	burst	burst
bring	brought	brought
lie	lay	lain
lay	laid	laid
get	got	got or gotten

An extensive list of irregular verbs can be found in Helpful Topics.

2.7.4 Indicative, Imperative and Subjunctive Moods

Mood is a set of verb forms expressing a particular attitude. There are three main types of mood in English:

⟹ **Indicative**   ⟹ **Imperative**   ⟹ **Subjunctive**

The indicative mood is the most common one, used to express factual statements.

I love playing the piano.

The imperative mood is used to express commands.

Please close the window immediately!

The subjunctive mood expresses possibilities and wishes.

If I were you, I would tell him my feelings.

The subjunctive is rarely used, but it is more often found in formal American usage than in British. The present subjunctive is very rare, having been overtaken by the present indicative, which it resembles in all parts except the third person singular: the subjunctive has no -s ending. The verb *to be*, however, has the form *be* for every person.

I'll call you if need *be*.

The past subjunctive is identical with the ordinary past tense, but again, the verb *to be* is different, having the form *were* for all persons.

If I *were* you, I would not do that.

Since the subjunctive expresses possibility, not fact, it is therefore found in

(1) Clauses beginning with *if, as if, though, as though* and

(2) After verbs expressing some kind of wish, recommendation, proposal, desire, regret, doubt, or demand.

The *if* (in subjunctive mood), *as if, though, as though* clauses express a condition that is NOT true.

Dependent Clause	Main Clause	Example
Present (True Condition)	Will/Can + Verb (base form)	**If you put your heart into it, you will be the winner.**
Past (Untrue Condition)	Would/Could + Verb (base form)	**If you put your heart into it, you could be the winner.**
Past Perfect (Untrue Condition)	Would have/Could have + Verb (past participle)	**If you had put your heart into it, you could have been the winner.**

When the subjective is used after verbs expressing some kind of wish, recommendation, proposal, desire, regret, doubt, or demand, there is a degree of uncertainty related to the final outcome.

Wrong

> She recommended that John *should* take the ferry.

> She recommended that John *takes* the ferry.

> She recommended that John *had taken* the ferry.

Correct

> She recommended that John *take* the ferry.

Note that you should ALWAYS just use the base form of the verb in such a subjunctive construction involving the *that* clause.

Regarding a list of words that are associated with the subjunctive mood, unfortunately, there's no hard and fast principle for it. This is what the linguists would call a lexical issue; the particular word and its meaning determine whether or not it can take an infinitive complement.

The following verbs can be used with a subjunctive that-clause:

> advise

> advocate

> ask

> beg

> decide

> decree

> demand

> desire

> dictate

> insist

> intend

mandate

move (in the parliamentary sense)

order

petition

propose

recommend

request

require

resolve

suggest

urge

vote

Of these, the following can ALSO take an infinitive, X to Y construction:

advise

ask

beg

order

petition

request

require

urge

The infinitive group is to some degree distinguished by their being directed at a person, rather than at a state of affairs.

2.7.5 Participle

There are several parts of the verb system which function as if they were different parts of speech (in the case of a participle, an adjective). In grammar, the PARTICIPLE is the term for two verb forms, the PRESENT PARTICIPLE (the "-ing" participle) and the PAST PARTICIPLE (the "-ed" participle, also ending in "-d' and "-t"). Both participles may be used like adjectives, but only if the participle indicates some sort of permanent characteristic: "running water", "the missing link", "lost property".

The PRESENT PARTICIPLE ends in "-ing" and is used in combination with the auxiliary "be" for the progressive continuous, as in: "am driving", "has been talking", etc.

The PAST PARTICIPLE ends in "-ed", "-d" or "-t" for all regular verbs and many irregular verbs, but many irregular verbs end in "-en" and "-n" (as in, "stolen" and "known") or with a change in the middle vowel (as in, "sung").

2.7.5.1 Present Participle

The present participle ends in *-ing*. Like an adjective, it may be used to form a predicate with the verb *to be*:

> Her feelings for Bob *were burgeoning* quickly.

> She *is stunning* in that dress.

Used as an adjective, it holds the normal adjectival position:

> Her *burgeoning* feelings for Bob surprised her.

> The *stunning* woman looked straight at me.

Participles are commonly found in phrases alongside the main part of the sentence:

> *Burgeoning* rapidly, *her feelings* for Bob rose to an untenable level.

If there is no appropriate noun, the sentence becomes nonsensical. The falsely assigned participle is known as 'dangling' or 'misrelated':

> **Wrong:** *Burgeoning* rapidly, *she* was soon unable to control her feelings for Bob.

As we will discuss in the Sentence Correction section, this is one of the most common errors on the GMAT, so learn to recognize a misplaced modifier (dangling participle), and you will have great success with these questions.

2.7.5.2 Past Participle

The past participle ends in *-(e)d* or *-t* in most verbs. A few archaic strong forms remain; these are verbs which make the past tense by changing the internal vowel, e.g., *write, wrote; see, saw*. These have participles that end in *-(e)n*, e.g. *written, seen*. The past participle forms a compound tense (perfect) with the addition of the verb *to have*. This denotes the perfected or completed action:

> I have *decided* to leave you.

It is useful to be able to recognize tenses in the Sentence Correction section, because another of the most common errors on the GMAT is changing tenses needlessly in the middle of a sentence. Make sure that the answer you select does not have a change of tense which is not justified by the meaning of the sentence.

Used adjectivally, however, the past participle may also form a predicate with the verb *to be*.

> I *have slain* you.

> You *are slain*.

As with the present participle, the past participle must be related to its proper noun when forming a modifying phrase:

> *Embarrassed* by her faux pas, *Ellen* left the room.

If the participle is misrelated (misplaced), comic results will occur:

> **Wrong:** *Covered* with aluminum foil, I popped the lasagna into the oven.

> (Here it is me, and not the lasagna, that is covered with aluminum foil!)

2.7.5.3 Special Situations

Absolute participle constructions are rare, and normally consist of noun and participle
- the noun to which the participle refers is actually present, although it does not have
a function in the rest of the sentence:

> *The game being over*, the players all went home.

> *Weather permitting*, the wedding will be held outdoors.

A similar construction has the preposition *with*:

> I returned to school *with my essay revised*.

A few participles have virtually become prepositions in their own right. These are:

> *barring, considering, excepting, including, owing (to), regarding, respecting, seeing, touching*;

and the past forms,

> *excepted, provided, given*.

Student Notes:

2.7.6 Gerund & Infinitive

The GERUND is a verbal noun, in English a word ending in "-ing". In fact, many gram-
merians of English use the term PARTICIPLE to include the gerund. Take the word
"visiting" in the sentence: "They appreciate my visiting their parents regularly."

Like participles, gerunds are verbal elements which take on the role of another part of
speech (in this case, that of a noun).

More common is the form ending in *-ing*, and this is identical with the form of the
present participle. The two are distinguished only by function:

> Taking this route was a mistake. (subject, *taking*)

> Why are we going this way? (participle, *going*)

There is no preferred version, but it is important to maintain parallelism in your constructions.

If an ordinary noun can be substituted for the *-ing* form, then it is a gerund, e.g.,

> *Taking it* was the fun part.

> *Its capture* was the fun part.

The gerund retains its verbal function by taking an object:

> *Owning a monkey* is very unconventional.

Less commonly, the noun function dictates the form:

The wearing of pink by red-headed people is a major fashion crime. (Wearing pink …)

Where a noun or pronoun is used with a gerund, it should be in the possessive case:

My admonishing him will not change his mind.

It was *his winning* that bothered me, not *my losing*.

I can't stand *my mother's telling* my friends embarrassing stories about me.

Any word may be used as an attributive (adjective) if placed before a noun. A gerund may be used this way (called a *gerundive*); its form is identical with the present participle, but the meaning will be different:

A *building* reputation - participle (a reputation that is building)

Some *building* blocks - gerund (blocks for building with)

A *working* appliance - participle (an appliance that works)

working papers - gerund (papers which allow you to work)

The infinitive form of a verb has a "to" proceeding it:

to + verb

The infinitive form may be used in this function:

To err is human, to forgive, divine.

(= Error is human, forgiveness, divine.)

Care must be taken not to use a mixture of the two forms:

Talking to him was one thing, but kissing him was entirely another!

To talk to him was one thing, but to kiss him was entirely another!

Not: Talking to him was one thing, but to kiss him was entirely another!

Do avoid inserting a word or a phrase between the to and the verb in the infinitive form. This error is known as a *split infinitive*.

Wrong

I asked him to quickly clean the table.

Correct

I asked him to clean the table quickly.

Student Notes:

2.8 Conjunction

Conjunctions are used to connect words or constructions. You should simply keep in mind that the most common conjunctions are AND, BUT, OR, which are used to connect units (nouns, phrases, gerunds, and clauses) of equal status and function. The other conjunctions, BECAUSE, IF, ALTHOUGH, AS, connect a subordinate clause to its superordinate clause, as in "We did it BECAUSE he told us to."

Generally don't begin sentences with conjunctions- *however* is better than *but* for this, but it goes best after semicolons. Or use the adverb *instead*.

Correlative expressions such as *either/or, neither/nor, both/and, not only/but also* and *not/but* should all correlate ideas expressed with the same grammatical construction. Special care has to be taken with clauses: only clauses of the same kind can be joined with a conjunction. Similarly, a phrase cannot be joined to a clause.

American usage is extremely fastidious in making constructions parallel, and this is another one of the common tricks in the Sentence Correction questions. Keep a lookout for conjunctions and lists, and you will be able to catch these errors.

2.9 Helpful Topics

2.9.1 Punctuation

Punctuation is the practice in writing of using a set of marks to regulate texts and clarify their meanings, mainly by separating or linking words, phrases and clauses. Currently, punctuation is not used as heavily as in the past. Punctuation styles vary from individual, newspaper to newspaper and press to press, in terms of what they consider necessary.

Improper punctuation can create ambiguities or misunderstandings in writing, especially when the comma is misused. For example, consider the following examples:

> "They did not go, because they were lazy." In this case, the people in question did not go for one reason: "because they were lazy." But consider the sentence again:

> "They did not go because they were lazy." In this case, without the comma, the people probably DID go, but not because they were lazy, for some other reason (they did not go because they were lazy, they went because they were tired).

Periods and Commas

(1) **Periods and Commas**: the most common form of punctuation. The period ends a sentence, whereas the comma marks out associated words within sentences. Commas are used for pauses, prepositional phrases, and appositive clauses offset from the rest of the sentence to rename a proper noun (Thomas, a baker,); they are the rest stop in English language.

(2) **Colons, Semicolons, and Dashes (or Hypens)**: Many people avoid the use of colon and semicolon, because of uncertainty as to their precise uses. In less formal writing, the dash is often used to take the place of both the colon and the semi-colon. The rule is that both colons and semicolons must follow a complete independent

clause. A semicolon must be followed by another complete clause, either dependent or independent. A colon may be followed by a list or phrase, or by a complete clause.

- The APOSTROPHE (') used to show possession: Those books are Thomas's books.

- The COLON (:) is normally used in a sentence to lead from one idea to its consequences or logical continuation. The colon is used to lead from one thought to another.

- The SEMICOLON (;) is normally used to link two parallel statements.

- Consider the following examples:

  - COLON: "There was no truth in the accusation: they rejected it utterly."

    * Points to a cause/effect relationship, as a result of ...

  - SEMICOLON: "There was no truth in the accusation; it was totally false." (Here two parallel statements are linked "no truth" and "totally false". In the COLON example, the consequence is stated after the insertion of the colon).

    * Re-states initial premise, creates relation between disparate parts

    * Technically these sentences could be broken down into two separate sentences and they would remain grammatically sound. But two sentences here would suggest separateness (which in speech the voice would convey with a longer pause) that is not always appropriate.

- HYPHENS or DASHES: The hyphen or dash is perhaps most important in order to avoid ambiguity, and is used to link words. Consider the following example:

  - "Fifty-odd people" and "Fifty odd people". When the hyphen is used, the passage means "approximately fifty people." But the second passage means "fifty strange people".

Otherwise, the use of the hyphen is declining. It was formerly used to separate vowels (co-ordinate, make-up), but this practice is disappearing.

For example:

House plant → house-plant → houseplant

2.9.2   List of Irregular Verbs

To correctly use the verbs in different tense forms, please study the list carefully.

Base Form	Past Tense	Past Participle
Awake	Awaked; awoke	Awaked; awoken
Be	Was/Were	Been
Beat	Beat	Beat; beaten
Become	Became	Become
Begin	Began	Begun
Bend	Bent	Bent
Bite	Bit	Bitten
Bleed	Bled	Bled
Blow	Blew	Blown
Break	Broke	Broken
Bring	Brought	Brought
Build	Built	Built
Burst	Burst	Burst
Buy	Bought	Bought
Catch	Caught	Caught
Choose	Chose	Chosen
Come	Came	Come
Cost	Cost	Cost
Cut	Cut	Cut
Deal	Dealt	Dealt
Dig	Dug	Dug
Dive	Dived; dove	Dived
Do	Did	Done
Draw	Drew	Drawn
Dream	Dreamed; dreamt	Dreamed; dreamt
Drink	Drank	Drunk
Drive	Drove	Driven
Eat	Ate	Eaten
Fall	Fell	Fallen
Feed	Fed	Fed
Feel	Felt	Felt
Fight	Fought	Fought
Find	Found	Found
Fit	Fitted; fit	Fitted; fit
Fly	Flew	Flown
Forget	Forgot	Forgotten
Freeze	Froze	Frozen
Get	Got	Gotten; got
Give	Gave	Given
Go	Went	Gone
Grow	Grew	Grown

Base Form	Past Tense	Past Participle
Hang (an object)	Hung	Hung
Hang (a person)	Hanged	Hanged
Hear	Heard	Heard
Hide	Hid	Hidden; hid
Hit	Hit	Hit
Hold	Held	Held
Hurt	Hurt	Hurt
Keep	Kept	Kept
Kneel	Knelt; kneeled	Knelt; kneeled
Knit	Knit; knitted	Knit; knitted
Know	Knew	Known
Lay (put down)	Laid	Laid
Lead	Led	Led
Lean	Leaned	Leaned
Leave	Left	Left
Lend	Lent	Lent
Let	Let	Let
Lie (recline)	Lay	Lain
Light	Lighted; lit	Lighted; lit
Lose	Lost	Lost
Make	Made	Made
Mean	Meant	Meant
Meet	Met	Met
Pay	Paid	Paid
Prove	Proved	Proved; proven
Put	Put	Put
Quit	Quit; quitted	Quit; quitted
Read	Read	Read
Rid	Rid; ridden	Rid; ridden
Ride	Rode	Ridden
Ring	Rang	Rung
Run	Ran	Run
Say	Said	Said
See	Saw	Seen
Sell	Sold	Sold
Send	Sent	Sent
Set	Set	Set
Shake	Shook	Shaken
Shine	Shone; shined (polish)	Shone; shined (polish)

Base Form	Past Tense	Past Participle
Shoot	Shot	Shot
Show	Showed	Showed; shown
Shrink	Shrank	Shrunk
Shut	Shut	Shut
Sit	Sat	Sat
Sleep	Slept	Slept
Slide	Slid	Slid
Speak	Spoke	Spoken
Speed	Sped; speeded	Sped; speeded
Spend	Spent	Spent
Spin	Spun	Spun
Spring	Sprang	Sprung
Stand	Stood	Stood
Steal	Stole	Stolen
Stick	Stuck	Stuck
Sting	Stung	Stung
Strike	Struck	Struck; stricken
Swear	Swore	Sworn
Swim	Swam	Swum
Swing	Swung	Swung
Take	Took	Taken
Teach	Taught	Taught
Tear	Tore	Torn
Tell	Told	Told
Think	Thought	Thought
Throw	Threw	Thrown
Wake	Waked; woke	Waked; woken
Wear	Wore	Worn
Win	Won	Won
Wring	Wrung	Wrung
Write	Wrote	Written

2.9.3 Words Frequently Confused

The following words are often misused, even by experienced writers:

accumulative, cumulative

adverse, averse

affect, effect

affluent, effluent

allusion, illusion, delusion
alternate, alternative

amiable, amicable, amenable

anomaly, analogy

apposite, opposite

appraise, apprise
ascent, assent, accent

belated, elated

beneficent, benevolent

biannual, biennial

censer, censor, censure

colloquy, obloquy

complement, compliment

contemptuous, contemptible

continual, continuous, contiguous

credible, credulous

decry, descry

deduce, deduct

deficient, defective

denote, connote

deprecate, depreciate

dependent, dependant

derisive, derisory

devolve, evolve
digress, regress

disburse, disperse

discrete, discreet

disquisition, inquisition

economic, economical

edible, eatable

efficient, effectual, effective

eject, inject

elusive, illusive

erotic, exotic

erupt, disrupt

euphony, cacophony

fallacious, fallible

fictitious, factitious

further, farther

grouchy, grungy

historic, historical

hoard, horde
homogenous, homogeneous

human, humane

hypercritical, hypocritical

inchoate, chaotic

induce, indict

ineligible, illegible

ingenious, ingenuous

insidious, invidious

intermediate, intermediary

introspection, retrospection

judicial, judicious

lie, lay

lightening, lightning

luxurious, luxuriant

monitory, monetary

negligible, negligent

notable, notorious

observance, observation
obtrude, intrude

ordinance, ordnance

oral, aural

overt, covert

peaceful, peaceable

perspective, perceptive

perspicacious, perspicuous

precipitate, precipitous

precede, proceed

preclude, prelude

prescribe, proscribe

principle, principal

prospective, prosperous

raise, rise

reputed, imputed

resource, recourse

salutary, salubrious

seasonal, seasonable
spasmodic, sporadic

tacit, taciturn

temperature, temperament

temporize, extemporize

tortuous, torturous

uninterested, disinterested

urban, urbane

veracious, voracious

vocation, avocation

If you think you may not know the difference between any of these pairs, or would like to brush up on the meanings of any of these words, please ask your instructor to clarify them, or look them up in a dictionary before your test date.
Student Notes:

2.9.4 American vs. British Usage

American spelling often differs from British usage, but this is **not** one of the factors tested in the GMAT examination. Examples include:

· The use of *-or* instead of British *-our*, e.g., *color, harbor, favor*, and the use of *-er* for *-re*, e.g., *center, fiber, theater*.

· The final or internal *e* is dropped in *ax, acknowledgment, judgment, jewelry.* Other modifications include: *plow, wagon, check* (cheque), *pajamas, gray, mold, program, draft, marvelous, traveler.*

· The double *-ll* is retained in *skillful, fulfill, install*; the endings *-ise, -isation,* are written, *-ize, -zation.*

If such American spelling forms appear in the sentences for correction, no alternatives will be given, so that there is in fact no problem.

Some nouns have given rise to new usages, such as *service*, and this is acceptable in both American and British English. Others are not, e.g., *suspicion* for 'suspect'. Again, the presence of other forms in the choices given will indicate whether this usage is to be considered non-standard or not. The word *loan* is used only as a noun in British English, but is an acceptable verb form in American English.

Standard American words frequently differ from their British equivalents -

Frequently Used in America	Frequently Used in Britain
apartment	flat
boardwalk	promenade
bug	insect
drapes	curtains
elevator	lift
fall	autumn
fix a flat	change a tire
garbage can, ashcan	dustbin
gas	petrol
hardware store	ironmonger's
mad	angry
peek	peer, glimpse
pillow	cushion
pitcher	jug
railroad	used as a verb
round trip	return trip
salesgirl	shop assistant
sidewalk	pavement
sick	ill, diseased
smokestack	chimney

There are many more of these, but as these are not 'diction' errors, no alternative version will be given among the multiple choice answers in the Sentence Correction section.

Student Notes:

2.9.5 Standard vs. Non-standard Usage

There are many American expressions that do not meet standard requirements; most of these are easily recognized, but some may raise doubts. As a general rule, *kind of* and *sort of* are to be avoided altogether:

I was *sort of* hurt by that.

If used adjectivally - and this would be possible - *kind of* does not have an article:

I thought I saw you with some *kind of* food.

The expression *those (these) kind of things* is particularily offensive, since *kind* and *sort* are singular and would properly be preceded by *that* or *this*. Similarly, the ending *-s* should never be attached to compounds of *-where*, e.g., *somewhere*. The *-s* ending is, however to be found in the compounds of *-ways*, e.g., *always, sideways, longways, lengthways*, but *anyways* and *ways* are nonstandard forms, as are *someway, noway* and *nohow*. Nonstandard also are the expressions *can't seem to*, for 'seem unable to' and *go to*, meaning 'intend'. *Any* should not be used adverbially:

Wrong: I don't think I hurt him *any*.

The correct expression is *at all*.

Adjectives should not be used as adverbs:

Wrong: We agreed on the specifics *some*; (use *some* for 'somewhat')

Wrong: I thought my plan would *sure* succeed; (use *sure* for 'surely', 'certainly'.)

Wrong: I noticed a guy who was *real* cute standing outside; (use *real* for 'really'.)

Non-standard usages would include verbs used as nouns, as in *eats* or *invite* (invitation), prepositions used in conjunctions, or *without* for 'unless':

Wrong: I won't come along *without* you apologize.

or *on account* for 'because':

Wrong: I liked him *on account* he made me toys and things.

All should not be followed by *of* unless a pronoun follows:

I hate *all those people*.

I hate *all of you*!

Other nonstandard expressions include:

Nonstandard	**Standard**
be at	be
both alike	either 'both' or 'alike'
bring	take
equally near	equally
have a loan of	borrow
have got	have
human	human being
in back of	behind
inside of	within
lose out	lose
no account, no good	worthless
no place	nowhere
nowhere near	not nearly
off of	from or completely
out loud	aloud
outside of	outside or except
over with	ended
over with	over
plenty, mighty	very

Student Notes:

Student Notes:

Chapter 3

Sentence Correction

The Grammar Review in the previous section touches on nearly all of the flaws you are likely to encounter in Sentence Correction questions on the GMAT.

The Sentence Correction section tests your knowledge of written English grammar by asking you which of the five choices best expresses an idea or relationship. This section gives you a sentence that may or may not contain errors of grammar or usage. You must select either the answer that best corrects the sentence or the answer stating that the sentence is correct as is. The questions will require you to be familiar with the stylistic conventions and grammatical rules of standard written English and to demonstrate your ability to improve incorrect or ineffective expressions.

This section tests two broad aspects of language proficiency:

- · Correct expression

- · Effective expression

- · Proper Diction

A correct sentence is grammatically correct and structurally soun It conforms to all the rules of standard written English such as subject-verb agreement, verb tense consistency, modifier reference and position, idiomatic expressions and parallel construction.

In addition to being correct, a sentence needs to be effective. It should express an idea or relationship clearly and concisely, as well as grammatically. A best choice should have no superfluous words or unnecessarily complicated expressions. This does not mean that the shortest choice is always the best answer. Proper diction is another important part of effectiveness. It refers to the standard dictionary meanings of words and the appropriateness of words in context. In evaluating the diction of a sentence, you must be able to recognize whether the words are well-selected, correctly presented, and suitable for the context.

One common error that test takers often make in the Sentence Correction section is choosing an answer that sounds good. Do not go on with your gut feeling in this section. Remember your grammar and look for errors in construction (e.g., noun-verb agreement) and eliminate answers that you are sure are incorrect.

3.1 How to Tackle

The following is a step by step process that you should follow to tackle Sentence Correction questions:

(1) **Read the whole sentence for structure and content.**

You have to understand the entire sentence to be able to pick the best choice later. You should read the sentence for meaning as well as structure. Two questions you should ask yourself are:

- · What is the author trying to say?

  Some answers to GMAT questions are grammatically correct but change the meaning of the sentence. Such answers are wrong.

- · What is the structure of the sentence?

  As you read the sentence, try to identify the subject and verb, prepositions, conjunctions, and participles. These parts of speech are associated with the common errors found in Sentence Correction questions. You won't have to identify the grammatical function of each word, phrase and clause in the sentence, but please just be familiar with the common errors and watch for **signals** (which we will discuss later) that the question is testing a specific error.

(2) **Try to predict the correct answer.**

You may already have an idea of how to correct the sentence. Before you plunge into the answers for the question, try to predict what the correct answer is going to be.

For example, in the sentence "Shelly <u>have three items</u> in her pocket," the correct answer choice is likely to contain the verb "has".

While your ability to predict the correct answer will improve with practice, you will not be able to correctly predict the correct answer choice all the time.

(3) **Don't read the first answer choice.**

Reading the first answer choice is **always** a waste of your time. You have already read it in the original sentence! The first answer choice is **always** the same as the underlined portion of the original sentence.

Remember that 1 of 5 Sentence Correction questions contain no error. If you think that the original sentence is correct, then go ahead and scan through answers 2-5, but do not become flustered if none of the answers are correct. After all **20% of the Sentence Correction problems need no correction**.

(4) **Scan through the answer choices.**

Each Sentence Correction problem in the GMAT is created usually with two or three different possible errors where you have to pay attention. The various combinations of these possible errors result in the options you are given.

If you have predicted the correct answer, you need only to identify the choice which matches your prediction. Sometimes you will find an exact match, but more often you will be able to narrow the answer choices to two or three.

If you were not able to predict the correct answer, look for evidence in the answer choices to determine what is being tested by the question in order to pick the best answer. For example, if more than one answer choice is similar except for a few words, your investigation should begin with the answers that are similar.

When you have found the parts of the sentence being varied, look for evidence in the remaining part of the sentence to determine which option to choose. Start with whatever is dictated by the unchanging part of the sentence. For example, if a verb is provided in singular and plural forms, find the subject of the sentence.

(5) **Eliminate wrong answers.**

By now, you should have an idea of what answers are grammatically or stylistically incorrect. Eliminate these answers and focus on the differences among the remaining choices.

(6) **Read your choice back into the sentence.**

Remember that the GMAT test-writers will often create answer choices which are grammatically correct, but either change the meaning of the sentence or are not stylistically the best answer. Since the GMAT tests not only grammar but also efficiency and effectiveness of communication, you have to look for redundancy, ambiguity, and uncommon or confusing expressions.

Reading your choice back into the sentence will help you decide which answer communicates the meaning of the sentence most effectively and prevent you from making careless errors.

3.2   Special Advice

Sentence Correction accounts for 13-16 of the 41 questions in the verbal section of the GMAT. While you have an average of almost 2 minutes to answer each question on the verbal section, we recommend that you spend less time on each Sentence Correction question. **In fact, we recommend that you should practice getting your speed down to one minute or less!**
Answering Sentence Correction questions rapidly will allow you to "bank" time in the verbal section that you can use to concentrate on a difficult reading comprehension passage or to focus on a challenging critical reasoning question. Remember that the verbal section is the last section on the GMAT, and your endurance is likely to be fading at this point in the test. You may find that you need a few moments of the additional time you have saved to recover your energy to push through to the last question.
The Sentence Correction questions in the GMAT have several types of errors, most of which reoccur frequently throughout this section of the test. A close and thorough study of Manhattan Review's Grammar Review will help you rapidly identify and correct these errors. We often recommend to students who are pressed for preparation time that they spend the lion's share of their studies on Sentence Correction. The time you spend concentrating on Sentence Correction and practicing spotting the common errors quickly is among the most productive time you may spend studying for the GMAT.

While trying to answer each question correctly in such a short amount of time may seem daunting, practicing the steps outlined earlier will help you answer the questions efficiently, effectively and most important, correctly.

Student Notes:

3.3 Common Errors and Tested Topics

3.3.1 Misplaced Modifiers (and Dangling Participles)

Modifiers are phrases that modify another part of the sentence. In order to be correct, the modifying phrase must be as close as possible to what it modifies. For example:

Disgusting and pus-filled, Enrico nursed his festering wound.

In this example it sounds as if Enrico is disgusting and pus-filled, rather than his wound. As soon as you read this sentence, you should immediately realize that the correct answer choice will place *disgusting and pus-filled* as close as possible to wound. To wit:

Enrico nursed his *disgusting and pus-filled* festering wound.

Signals

· An introductory phrase is a common signal of a Misplaced Modifier.

· Any modifying phrase which is not close to what it modifies may also indicate this error.

Another example

Career switchers often schedule interviews with high-level managers, believing that the insight of professionals will help narrow down the many choices of careers available to graduating MBAs.

(A) Career switchers often schedule interviews with high-level managers, believing that the insight of professionals will help narrow down the many choices of careers available to graduating MBAs

(B) Career switchers, believing that the insight of professionals will help narrow down the many choices of careers available to graduating MBAs, often schedule interviews with high-level managers

(C) Career switchers believing that scheduling interviews with the insight of high-level professional managers will help narrow down the many choices of careers available to graduating MBAs

(D) Career switchers, believing that interviews with high-level managers whose insight will help narrow down the many choices of careers available to graduating MBAs, often schedule them

(E) Career switchers often schedule interviews to narrow down the many choices of careers available to graduating MBAs, believing that the insight of professionals with high-level managers will help them

3.3.2 Agreement (Concord)

A very common Sentence Correction error centers on the agreement between the subject of a sentence and the verb. The subject and verb must agree in number, that is, a plural verb must have a plural subject and a singular verb must have a singular subject. This is particularly important with *of* constructions:

A *flock* of birds, flying south for the winter, *was* above us.

Another example:

My *group* of fourth graders *are* so well behaved.

The singular subject group demands the singular verb is. Thus the corrected sentence should read:

My *group* of fourth graders *is* so well behaved.

If the verb is inverted, care must be taken to find the subject:

I journeyed to the graveyard *where once stood my father's tomb.*

Agreement is based on formal grammar, and plurals do not depend on meaning but on the grammatical relationships between words. Two single subjects joined by *and* take a plural verb, but an addition in parentheses, such as *as well as, not to mention,* takes a singular verb.

Signals

· Collective nouns such as team, audience, staff, family, public or committee are singular.

· An intervening phrase which separates the noun from the verb is used to confuse the unwary test-taker.

· A sentence structure with the verb before the subject may indicate an Agreement error.

· A conjunction such as and; either/or; neither/nor, can be used as a trap.

3.3.3 Tense

Many GMAT questions center upon the relationships between tenses. While the tenses in a sentence do not have to be the same, they must relate to each other in a way that makes the sequence of actions clear to the reader. The term sequence of tenses refers to the rules which govern how we alter verb tenses to make clear that all events, past, present or future, are not simultaneous.

> As soon as I *hear* the dog bark, I *knew* you *were* at the door.

The above sentence sets forth a likely condition anticipated by the speaker. The use of the past tense is incorrect. The sentence may be corrected thus:

> As soon as I *hear* the dog bark, I *will* know you *are* at the door.

In the above example, the future tense makes clear that the dog's barking is anticipated by the speaker.

Errors in sequence of tenses often occur with the perfect tenses, all of which are formed by adding an auxiliary or auxiliaries to the past participle, the third principal part.

Some common auxiliaries are "had", "has", and "have". They are used with the past participle to form perfect tenses.

Unfortunately, the rules governing sequence of tenses are a bit of a jumble. Often you will have to rely on your ear and common sense to guide you with these questions. But below are some guidelines you can use in order to sort out what the correct sentence should look like.

- In complex sentences, the tense of the verb in the main clause governs the tenses of the verbs in subsequent or dependent clauses.

Tense in Main Clause	Purpose of Dependent Clause	Tense In Dependent Clause	Example
Present	To show same-time action	Simple Present	I am eager to go for a walk because I enjoy exercise.
-	To show earlier action	Simple Past	He feels that she made a mistake last year.
-	To show a period of time extending from some point in the past to the present	Present Perfect	The congregation believes that it has selected a suitable preacher.
-	To show action to come	Future	My teacher says that he will grade the test next week.
Simple Past	To show another completed past action	Simple Past	She cooked the salmon because she knew it was fresh.
-	To show an earlier action	Past Perfect	He cooked the salmon well because he had attended culinary school.
-	To state a general truth	Simple Present	Copernicus believed that the universe is like a giant clock.
Present Perfect	To show an earlier action	Simple Past	The lawyer has handled many cases since he passed the bar.
-	To show action happening at the same time	Present Perfect	She has grown a foot because she has taken steroids.
Past Perfect	For any purpose	Simple Past	The bird had flown for miles before it landed.
Future	To show action happening at the same time	Simple Present	I will be a senator if they vote for me.
-	To show an earlier action	Simple Past	You will go to the concert if you waited in line.
-	To show future action earlier than the action of the independent clause	Present Perfect	My grandmother will finish the puzzle soon if her dog has not eaten the pieces.
Future Perfect	For any purpose	Simple Present or Present Perfect	The factory will have produced many widgets long before it closes. The factory will have produced many widgets long before it has closed.

Do not confuse between the present perfect ("has walked") and the past perfect ("had walked"). While both verbs convey past action, the present perfect verb actually represents present tense.

The future tense makes clear that the dog's barking is anticipated by the speaker.
Signals

- Several actions occurring in different time frames.

- Multiple tenses.

Another example
When he phones her, <u>she tells him to stop calling, but he acted as if he had not understood her.</u>

(A)   she tells him to stop calling, but he acted as if he had not understood her.

(B)   she told him to stop calling, but he acted as if he had not understood her.

(C)   she tells him to stop calling, but he acts as if he did not understood her.

(D)   she tells him to stop calling, but he acts as if he has not understood her.

(E)   she tells him to stop calling, but he acted as if he does not understand her.

3.3.4   Faulty Parallelism

Parallelism is the most mathematical of the errors tested on the GMAT. Just as the expressions on each side of an algebraic equation must be equivalent, so too must the parts of speech on either side of a conjunction be the same. By thinking about a conjunction in a sentence as an equal sign, you can identify and correct this error.
For example:

Which do you like best, *to swim, a drive, or jogging*?

Predicting the correct answer for these types of errors presents some difficulty as often there is more than one way of restating the sentence correctly. For example the previous sentence may be corrected in three different ways:

Which do you like best, *to swim, to drive, or to jog*?

Which do you like best, *a swim, a drive, or a jog*?

Which do you like best, *swimming, driving, or jogging*?

Any of the above is correct as long as the words or phrases connected by the conjunction *or* are the same part of speech.
Signals

- Items in a list.

- Long phrases or clauses connected by a conjunction.

Another example
Our firm is best suited to undertake the project because we have <u>the financial wherewithal, vast experience undertaking similar projects, and can use our large employee base - all of which is necessary</u> to complete the work on-time and under-budget.

(A)   the financial wherewithal, vast experience undertaking similar projects, and can use our large employee base - all of which is necessary

(B)   the financial wherewithal, vast experience undertaking similar projects, and a large employee base - all necessary

(C)   the financial wherewithal, vast experience undertaking similar projects, and a large employee base - all of whom are necessary

(D)   the financial wherewithal, vast experience undertaking similar projects, and can use our large employee base necessary

(E)   the financial wherewithal, vast experience undertaking similar projects, and can use our large employee base since they are necessary

3.3.5   Comparisons

Comparisons are a first cousin of Parallelism. Frequently a sentence with a comparison will appear at first glance to be correct but will actually compare two or more elements which are not expressed in similar form. For example:

The judge of the baking contest liked *the pastry* Sally made better than *Bob*.
In this sentence, the judge is evaluating the comparative merits of Sally's pastry and Bob himself. Put it in another way, he is comparing Sally's pastry to Bob, rather than comparing Sally's pastry to Bob's pastry. The correct way of expressing the idea is thus:

The judge of the baking contest liked *Sally's pastry* better than *Bob's*.
Signals

· Key words such as than, like, unlike, as, compared to, more than, and less than should alert you to check what is being compared in the sentence.

Another example
Unlike its competitors, Globex and MondoCorp, the revenues of Galactic Enterprises increased by cornering the widget market in the fourth quarter, thus making Galactic Enterprises the world's most profitable company and a darling of Wall Street.

(A)   its competitors, Globex and MondoCorp, the revenues of Galactic Enterprises increased by cornering the widget market in the fourth quarter, thus making

(B)   Globex and MondoCorp, its competitors, the revenues of Galactic Enterprises increased by cornering the widget market in the fourth quarter, thus making

(C)   its competitors, Globex and MondoCorp, Galactic Enterprises increased its revenues by cornering the widget market in the fourth quarter, by making

(D)   Globex and MondoCorp, its competitors, Galactic Enterprises increased its revenues by cornering the widget market in the fourth quarter, thus making

(E)   its competitors, Globex and MondoCorp, the revenues of Galactic Enterprises cornered the widget market in the fourth quarter, thus making

3.3.6 Pronoun Agreement & Reference

Errors regarding pronouns fall into two broad categories: agreement and reference.

Agreement

Pronouns must agree with their antecedents in person, number and gender. If the antecedent is third person singular male, then the pronoun must be third person singular male as well. For example:

> In recent years, Fred has tried to lose *its* excess weight through numerous diets.

The correct sentence would read:

> In recent years, Fred has tried to lose *his* excess weight through numerous diets.

Reference

Pronoun reference errors occur when ambiguity exists as to the antecedent of the pronoun. Additionally, the pronouns must clearly refer to only one antecedent. The sentence must leave no doubt in the reader's mind as to what the pronoun refers. Sentences with multiple nouns are a classic signal of a pronoun reference error.

> The attorney argued that students who were denied the use of school facilities for political activities had lost *their* right of free assembly.

In the above sentence, the writer does not make clear to what *their* refers. It could refer to students, facilities or activities. The sentence must be constructed so that the reader has no doubt about the antecedent of the pronoun *their*:

> The attorney argued that students lost their right of free assembly when they were denied the use of school facilities for political activities.

Signals

· Several nouns preceding a pronoun.

Another example

The *Federalist Papers* is a compilation of articles written by Alexander Hamilton and James Madison, as well as a few by John Jay, <u>since each of them were</u> advocates of the Constitution.

(A) since each of them were

(B) since they were each

(C) since all of them were

(D) each of which was

(E) because all of the men were

3.3.7 Idioms, Usage, and Style

Sentence correction questions that revolve around idioms, usage and style generally test subtle errors in expression. Idiomatic expressions often have no basis in grammar or even logic but have been accepted into the language.

Especially for non-native speakers, some of the trickiest errors in this section are incorrect idioms. This includes using the wrong preposition with a verb, among many other things. Unfortunately, the only thing to do about this problem is practice, so do as many practice questions as possible and take note of any examples in which two different versions of an idiom are used. After you check your answers, make a list of the idioms you did not know and memorize them.

Native speakers often use idioms without thinking about the literal meaning of the words. For example:

> We finished the rest of the tasks *in one fell swoop.*

The expression in *one fell swoop* makes little sense literally, but English speakers recognize it as meaning all at once.

Some conventions of Standard English may seem nit-picky, but you should familiarize yourself with some rules which are commonly tested. For example:

Wrong

> When *compared to* Greg's ability to carry a tune, Marsha's musical skill is unimpressive.

The correct expression in this case is *compared with* because the items being compared are dissimilar: the relative musical abilities of Greg and Marsha. The construction using *compared with* points out the differences.

Correct

> When *compared with* Greg's ability to carry a tune, Marsha's musical skill is unimpressive.

Use *compared to* when illustrating similarities. For example:

> He *compared* his teacher *to* Bruce Greenwald, the esteemed professor famous for his Value Investing lectures at Columbia Business School.

> May I *compare* thee *to* a summer's day? (Shakespeare, Sonnet 18)

In sum, *Compare to* is used when things are being likened. *Compare with* is used when the comparison is more specific and implies differences.

Each . . . other refer to **two** entities; where more than two are concerned, use *one . . . another.*

> The two of them hated *each other* with a passion.

> The four of us looked at *one another* and laughed.

Student Notes:

3.3.7.1 GMAT Idiom List

a lot – The proper form is two words, not *alot*.

agree on – must be followed by the *-ing* form of a verb.

an instance of – is different in meaning from *an example of*. An *example* is one of a number of things while an *instance* is an *example* which proves or illustrates. People may be *examples* but never *instances*.

as vs. than – The words are not interchangeable. Use *as* for comparisons of similarity or equality and *than* for comparisons of degree or difference. Always use *than* with the comparative (-er) form of an adjective.

as good as or better than – is a cliché and should be avoided. Do not telescope a comparison of similarity - *as* with a comparison of degree - *than*. A better construction is to break the juxtaposition up into separate thoughts.

as ... as – is a grammatical way of expressing similarity: he is *as* tall *as* his sister.

such ... as – is grammatical when both words are used as prepositions in a comparison: *such* men *as* he. Avoid *as such* when meaning *in principle*.

based on – The phrasal verb *based on* is grammatical and can be used either actively or passively.

> The style of her cooking is *based on* Southern cuisine.

> She *bases* her thinking *on* sound logic.

depends on whether – The construction is generally accepted and is certainly preferable to *depends on if*.

> His fate *depends on whether* the governor calls back in time.

different from vs. different than (differ from)– Although strict grammarians say that *from* is the correct word to use after *different*, many authorities believe that *than* may be used in order to avoid elaborate constructions. In contrast, the authorities agree that *from* is the correct word when used with *differ*.

> He is a *different* man *than* he was in 1985. Compare to: He is a *different* man *from the man that* he was in 1985.

Identical with/to – *Identical* may be used with either preposition without changing the intended meaning.

no less a ... than – The expression is an accepted idiom meaning great or not less impressive.

not only/but also – *Not only* is **always** followed by *but also* in a sentence.

> The subways in summer are *not only* hot, *but also* humid.

regard as – The verb *regard* may be used with *as* and either an adjective or a noun.

> We *regard* George's ranting *as* silly. The tribe *regards* shaking hands *as* taboo.

> Do not use regard with an infinitive or *being*: He is regarded to be an expert; He is regarded as being an expert.

regardless – The word is correct. *Irregardless* is non-standard usage.

So ... as – The comparative construction may only be used in questions and negative statements. Otherwise, use *as ... as*.

Your house is not *so* large *as* mine.

So ... – Avoid the use of the appealing *so* as an intensifier. The weather is *so* delightful. Very would be a better choice. Similarly, when using *so* with a part participle, consider using *much* or *well* to qualify.

The car was *so much* damaged that it was not drivable.

Mary is *so well* suited to be an attorney.

3.3.7.2   Words Frequently Misused

Aggravate/annoy – *To aggravate* is to make a situation worse. *To annoy* is to irritate. In formal English, people cannot be aggravated, only annoyed.

When the Chairman of the Federal Reserve lowered interest rates, he *aggravated* the flailing economy and *annoyed* many Wall Street bankers.

Ago/since – *Ago* carries a thought from the present to the past. *Since* carries a thought from the past to the present.

It was twenty years *ago* that I first heard that song.

It has been twenty years *since* I first heard that song.

Among/between – Use *between* when comparing two items and *among* when comparing three or more

I was torn *between* studying finance and studying marketing.

After I was accepted into all three MBA programs, I had to choose *among* Harvard, Wharton and Columbia.

Amount/number – Use *amount* when referring to an uncountable noun and *number* when referring to a countable word.

There is a large *amount* of water in the ocean.

There are a large *number* of fish in the ocean.

Fewer/less – Use *fewer* when referring to a countable noun and *less* when referring to an uncountable noun. The usage of fewer/less is similar to amount/number.

The supermarket express lane is open to customers with ten items or *fewer*.

There is *less* rudeness at Dean and Deluca than at Fairway.

Good/well - When used as adjectives, good refers to morality or quality and well refers to health. However, only well can be used as adverb and good is always an adjective.

I feel *good* about my work.

I feel *well*.

I am *well*.

I'm doing *well*.

It is *good* to hear that you feel *well* today.

Imply/infer – *To imply* is to express a thought indirectly. *To infer* is to derive a conclusion indirectly.

While the politician never *implied* that he would raise taxes, the audience *inferred* that he would soon do so.

Like/as – Use *like* before a noun, or pronoun. Use *as* before a clause, adverb or prepositional phrase. *Like* is generally used as a preposition in such a context. *As* is generally used as an adverb while sometimes serving as a preposition with the meaning of "in the capacity of".

My mother's cheesecake tastes *like* glue.

I love frozen pizza because there is no other snack *like* it.

My mother's cheesecake tastes great, *as* a mother's cheesecake should.

There are times, *as* now, that learning grammar becomes important.

He golfed well again, *as* in the tournament last year.

He served *as* Captain in the navy.

Less than/under – *Less than* is the correct expression when making a comparison of number or amount. *Under* is limited to describing spatial relationships.

I will host the party if the guest list is *less than* fifty people.

More than/over – *More than* is the correct expression when making a comparison of number or amount. *Over* is limited to describing spatial relationships.

We processed *more than* 1,000 applications in one hour.

Student Notes:

3.4 What to Do If You Are Completely Stumped

Sometimes you may find yourself with one or more answer choices which seem to be correct. If you have followed Manhattan Review's six-step process for Sentence Correction and still find yourself to be lost, take a step back and think about the answer choices.

Read the answers back into the sentence, again

- You should have already done this, but if you are still stumped, do it again. Remember that a correct answer retains the meaning of the original sentence. You may be analyzing an answer choice which changes the idea which the author wished to convey. Make sure that word order has not been switched in the answer to suggest a different meaning.

Shorter is better

- Wordy or long-winded ways of expressing thoughts are often not the best means of expression. Sometimes the best answer is the one with the fewest words.

Eliminate answers with passive voice

· You will seldom encounter a correct answer that employs the use of the passive voice. While use of the passive voice is not in and of itself grammatically incorrect, expressing an idea actively is preferable. Given the choice between The ball was hit by me and I hit the ball, the latter is the better choice.

Avoid redundancy

· The best answer should be clear and concise. An answer which repeats elements of the sentence unnecessarily is incorrect.

Don't choose the answer with being

· Don't choose such answer if there are options which don't include the word being. Unless you are positive that being is a necessary and useful part of the sentence, it is probably just confusing the issue and is better left out.

If you review the rules discussed in the Grammar Review section and follow the six-steps for Sentence Correction questions, you should have little trouble identifying the best answer among your choices.

Answers to Prior Examples

3.3.1 Misplaced Modifier (B)	3.3.3 Tense (D)	3.3.4 Faulty Parallelism (B)
3.3.5 Comparison (D)	3.3.6 Pronoun Agreement & Reference (E)	

3.5 Detailed List of Typical Errors

Based on our close examination of all the Sentence Correction problems in the Official Guides and released old exams, we compiled the following list for your easy reference. **TIP: PLEASE FOCUS YOUR INITIAL ATTENTION ON BASIC GRAMMAR ELEMENTS ONLY - SUBJECT, VERB AND OBJECT.** Then examine the sentence in detail. That way you will not get bogged down by verbiage.

Goal I: Effectiveness of the Language

To achieve conciseness & clarity in a sentence, you should pick the choices that contain:

(1) a. No wordiness or fragment

(2) b. No redundancy

   Example: the remarkable growth in increased revenue

(3) c. No ambiguous double negative meanings

(4) d. No possibility for multiple interpretations of the sentence

(5) e. No change in meaning or intent

(6) Also, be suspicious of any answer choice containing:

   "being"
   "thing"

Goal II: Correctness of the Language

3.5.1 Modifiers

Be aware:

(1) **a. A participle at the start of a sentence must modify the subject of the sentence. Otherwise, it is a dangling participle.**

<u>Wrong</u>

Having read the book, there is no question the book is better than the film.

<u>Correct</u>

Having read the book, I have no doubt that the book is better than the film.

Also please pay attention to:

(1) **b. Misplaced modifying clause.**

<u>Wrong</u>

Whether baked or mashed, Tom loves potatoes.

<u>Correct</u>

Tom loves potatoes, whether baked or mashed.

(2) **c. Ambiguous modifying clause**

Example

People who jog frequently develop knee problems.

To eliminate ambiguity, you can change it to:

People develop knee problems if they jog frequently.
Or
People frequently develop knee problems if they jog.

(3) **d. Proximity between the modifier and the modified object**

Limiting modifiers (*just, only, hardly, almost*) must be used immediately before what they modify:

<u>Wrong</u>

The priest only sees children on Tuesdays between 4pm and 6pm.

<u>Correct depending on meaning</u>

The priest sees only children on Tuesdays between 4pm and 6pm.

-or-

The priest sees children only on Tuesdays between 4pm and 6pm.

-or-

The priest sees children on Tuesdays only between 4pm and 6pm.

(1) **e. Correct use of *that* vs *which* modifying clauses**

As relative pronouns the two words "*that*" and "*which*" are often interchangeable:

The house that/which stands on the hill is up for sale.

The school that/which they go to is just around the corner.

(When that or which is the object of a following verb, it can be omitted altogether, as in The school they go to . . . .)

When the relative clause adds incidental (non-essential) information rather than identifying the noun it follows, *which* is used and is preceded by a comma:

The house, *which* stands on the hill, is up for sale.

It means:

The house is up for sale. It happens to be on the hill.

When the relative clause identifies the noun it follows with essential information rather than adding incremental information, *that* is used without a comma:

The house *that* stands on the hill is up for sale.

It implies:

The house on the hill is up for sale. Not the house on the lake.

In other words, you can remove *which* from the sentence without affecting the meaning, while you have to keep *that* in the sentence to understand it fully.

(2) **f. Correct usage of the modifier, such as "little" vs. "few"**

(3) **g. Difference between adjective and adverb as modifiers**

3.5.2 Agreement

In grammar, Concord (also known as Agreement) refers to the relationship between units in such matters as number, person, and gender. Consider the following examples:

- "THEY did the work THEMSELVES" (number and person concord between THEY and THEMSELVES).

- "HE did the work HIMSELF" (number, person and gender concord between HE and HIMSELF).

- If there is no agreement, then grammatical errors occur. Consider the following example:

  "The apples is on the table." (Apples is plural; therefore, for concord to occur, the sentence should read: "The apples are on the table.")

A) Number and Person Concord: In Standard English, number concord is most significant between a singular and plural subject and its verb in the third person of the simple present tense:

"That book seems interesting" (singular BOOK agreeing with SEEMS), and

"Those books seem interesting" (plural BOOKS agreeing with SEEM).

Number concord requires that two related units must always both be singular or both be plural.

Both number and person concord are involved in the use of pronouns and possessives, as in "I hurt MYself," and "MY friends said THEY WERE COMING in THEIR car."

B) Gender Concord: Gender concord is an important part of the grammar of languages like German and French. In English, gender concord does not exist apart from personal and possessive pronouns, such as "Elizabeth injured HERself badly in the accident," and "Thomas lost HIS glasses." These errors are generally couched in a longer sentence, so the test taker is distracted and misses the simple error.

C) Subject-Verb Agreement: The easiest kind of trick the GMAT will pull is to give you subjects and verbs that do not agree in time or in number.

TIP: One of the things you always have to look out for is that the GMAT will throw in lots of extra words to confuse you about what subject the verb is referring to.

Example

> Although the sting of <u>brown honey locusts are rarely fatal, they cause painful flesh wounds.</u>

Please remember:

(1) **a. Certain words ending in "*s*" such as "*Diabetes*" and "*News*" are singular.**
Other examples include:

> two hundred dollars
>
> five hundred miles
>
> United States

(2) **b. Compound subject is plural.** Exception: "Romeo and Juliet" is a singular noun when it is referred to as a play.

(3) **c. "Each" and "Everyone" are singular.**

(4) **d. Collective nouns are singular.**
Common examples include group, audience, etc.

Note that if the subject of a sentence is an entire phrase or clause, you should use a singular verb, regardless of the plural words inside this phrase or clause.

Example

> Networking with professionals certainly helps a lot when you first start your career.

(5) **e. Indefinite Pronouns are singular.**
Examples: each, either, anything, everything, nothing, anyone, everyone, no one, neither, anybody, everybody, nobody

(6) **f. No verb should be missing in a sentence.**

(7) **g. Subject and verb should ALWAYS be in agreement.**

Singular	Plural
The number of	A number of
_____ together with _____ (as well as, combined with, etc)	_____ and _____
	_____ or _____

_____ nor _____

(verb agrees with nearer subject)

none, all, any, some
(depends on context; pay attention to the object after "of")

majority, minority
(depends on context)

(Singular when referring to the total group; plural when referred to many individual members of the group)

3.5.3   Verb Tense, Voice & Mood

Please remember to avoid:

(1) a. Inconsistent tense

(2) b. Passive voice

(3) c. Incorrect use of verbs in the subjunctive mood

3.5.4   Parallelism

Please pay attention to the inconsistent use of:

(1) a. Clauses

(2) b. Phrases (verb phrases, noun phrases, prepositional phrases, adjective phrases, etc.)

(3) c. Gerunds

(4) d. Infinitives (If an infinitive is repeated once in a list, it must be repeated each time.)

Wrong

I like to jog, swim and to run.

Correct

I like to jog, to swim and to run.

(Occasionally acceptable: I like to jog, swim and run.)

3.5.5   Comparisons

Please pay attention to the use of:

(1) a. *Like* vs. *As* vs. *Such As*

(2) b. *As Old As* vs. *Older Than*

(3) c. Illogical Comparison

(4) d. Ambiguous Comparison

3.5.6 Pronoun Agreement & Reference

Please remember:

(1) a. Antecedent and pronoun should be in agreement.

(2) b. No ambiguity with antecedent

(3) c. No missing antecedent

(4) d. Use of the relative pronoun should be correct

  · Which is for things only; Who/Whom for people only

  · Who vs Whom – nominative vs. objective case forms.

  · They/them is not correct as a singular pronoun, nor is it correct as a pronoun with no antecedent.

3.5.7 Idioms, Usage and Style

Here are some selected examples of common words and phrases tested on the GMAT.
From ____ to ____
Between ____ and ____
The same to ____ as to ____
No less ____ than ____
The more ____ the greater ____
Better served by ____ than by ____
Not only ____ but also ____
Both ____ and ____
Different from ____ (not "than" or "to")
Either ____ or ____
Neither ____ nor ____
Whether to do something or not
They do not know x or y (NOT x nor y)
Doubt that
At the urging of somebody
Between (2) vs Among (> 2)
Affect (verb) vs Effect (noun)
Assure (give an assurance) vs Ensure (make sure something happens) vs Insure (financially guarantee)
Equivalent in number (vs "as many as people")
A number of (not "numbers of")
Whether vs. If - "I had to decide whether", not "I had to decide if"

(1) Whether is typically used to introduce doubt regarding two equal possibilities or two alternatives.

We should try to have a dinner with them *whether* it's snowing or not.

He wonders *whether* it's worth the try.

She said she'd get here *whether* by train *or* by flight.

It is preferred to use "whether" over "if" when the word "if" is not used to signal a condition and instead takes the meaning of "whether". This is particularly true with the GMAT. Using "whether" exclusively avoids the possible confusion between different possible meanings of "if".

Wrong

I don't know *if* I am ready to take the test now and *if* I will ever be ready in the future.

Correct

I don't know *whether* I am ready to take the test now and *whether* I will ever be ready in the future.

"Despite" is not the same as "Although". "Despite" means 'with intention, in the face of an obstacle'.

(1) **Wrong**

Despite having 5% of the world's population, the USA uses 30% of the world's energy.

(2) **Correct**

Despite his poor education, he succeeded in becoming wealthy.

Idiomatic Prepositions:

based *on*

composed *by* meaning "created by" vs composed of meaning "made up of"

credit *with* (not credit to)

depend *on*

differ *with* (meaning "disagree with") vs differ *from* (meaning "be different from")

discourage *from* doing something/encourage to do something (from is a preposition here; to is the infinitive here)

prefer _____ *to* _____

prevent *from*

prohibit *from*

Idiomatic Phrases Involving or Omitting "As"

consider x y (not *to be* y)

defined *as*

depicted *as*

regard x *as* y

regarded *as*

think of x *as* y

view x *as* y

Idiomatic Phrases Involving or Omitting the Infinitive "to"

Help someone do something
Make someone do something
Enable someone to do something
Forbid x to do y
Words Associated with Subjunctive Mood in "that" Clause
Demand *that*
Mandate *that*
Request *that*
Require *that* something be (not are/is)
Different Applications Involving "use"

Use (verb):	I use a pencil to write.
Used to (*to* is the infinitive):	I used to teach every night.
Be used to something/doing something (*to* is preposition):	
	I am used to challenges.
	I am used to being challenged.

It + adjective
After verbs such as *believe, consider, feel, find, think,* we can use *it + adjective* before a "that" clause or the infinitive.

> I find *it* impulsive to talk to the CEO directly in an elevator without being introduced.

> He felt *it* dreadful that his wife was diagnosed with anemia.

Avoid Run-On Sentence
A run-on sentence consists of two or more main clauses that are run together **without** proper punctuation. People often speak in run-on sentences, but they make pauses and change their tone so others can understand them. But in writing, we must break our sentences into shorter units so that all the readers can understand us.
Wrong

> *It is nearly six o'clock we have not gone through all the practice problems yet.*

There are several acceptable ways to correct this:

· Insert a semicolon between the clauses:

> *It is nearly six o'clock; we have not gone through all the practice problems yet.*

· Write the two clauses as two separate sentences:

> *It is nearly six o'clock. We have not gone through all the practice problems yet.*

· Insert a comma and a conjunction between the clauses:

> *It is nearly six o'clock, and we have not gone through all the practice problems yet.*

3.6 Useful Examples

Here are some examples of the types of questions you will be faced with in the Sentence Correction section.

Q1. Unlike Lee Ang whose films transcend ideology, Zhang Yi Mou is frequently dismissed <u>with being merely a photographer</u> for a visually impressive production with little meaning.

(A) with merely being a photographer

(B) as being a photographer merely

(C) for being merely a photographer

(D) as a mere photographer

(E) merely for being a photographer

The problem with the sentence as it stands: <u>dismissed with</u> is not idiomatic, it should be dismissed as or dismissed for. These two idioms mean different things - you can be dismissed for something from a job, but by critics, etc. one is dismissed AS something. This leaves you with choices B and D. B includes the word <u>being</u>, which automatically makes it suspect. Also, it is the longer choice, which makes it less likely to be correct. The adverb <u>merely</u> is placed very far away from the verb, causing an awkward construction.
This makes D a better choice.
D is correct.

Q2. Once almost covered under centuries of debris, <u>skilled artisans have now restored some original famous paintings during the Italian Renaissance.</u>

(A) skilled artisans have now restored some original famous paintings during the Italian Renaissance.

(B) some original famous paintings during the Italian Renaissance now have been by skillful artisans restored.

(C) the restoration of some original famous paintings during the Italian Renaissance has been done by skilled artisans.

(D) skilled artisans during the Italian Renaissance have now restored some original famous paintings.

(E) some original famous paintings during the Italian Renaissance have now been restored by skilled artisans.

What was covered? Some original famous paintings. The rest are like certain garnishes in a cocktail.
With modifying phrases at the beginning of the sentence, just determine what is being modified and select the answer which places that item directly after the phrase. Which have the correct opening? *B* *E*
B needlessly separates subject from verb, creating a very awkward construction.
This makes *E* the better choice.

Example
Janowitz, as other writers in New York City, considered Woolf as one of the foremost female modernist literary figures of the twentieth century.
2 mistakes:
Like vs. As in the first part (Janowitz like other artists...)
The second "As" is unnecessary (consider as is not idiomatic).

Another Example
In many rural provinces, the so-called party leaders are more powerful, wealthy and wield more influence as any other illicit group.
2 mistakes:
For sake of parallelism, third item in the list should be an adjective, not a verb phrase
It should be "more than", not "more as".

Q3. With centuries of seasonal roaming in search of pasture for their herds or food and water, the Nomads still found the goal of a bawdy, prolonged adventure an elusive one.

(A) With

(B) Following

(C) Despite

(D) Having spent

(E) As a result of

C is the best choice to indicate the emphasis of the Nomads' unchanging mentality after all the journeys.

Q4. The uniformized set of characters, which some historians date in the late Qing dynasty, was the key to the sustainability and prosperity of the Chinese culture over thousands of years.

(A) The uniformized set of characters, which some historians date

(B) The uniformized set of characters, which some historians have thought to occur

(C) Uniformizing the set of characters, dated by some historians at

(D) The uniformization of a set of characters, thought by some historians to have occurred

(E) The set of characters' uniformization, dated by some historians to have been

Before we look at the answers, let's answer the question: what is occurring? Historians are dating something. What are they dating? Not the uniformized set of characters itself, but the time when the characters became uniformized (the uniformization of the characters).
Therefore the correct answer must be *D*.

Student Notes:

Chapter 4

Critical Reasoning

The Critical Reasoning section tests your ability to make arguments, evaluate arguments, draw conclusions, and formulate or assess chains of reasoning. Luckily for you, this part is very similar in content to the Analytical Writing Assessment. In the majority of cases, the same fallacies you already know from the AWA are also hidden in this part.

Each question consists of a statement, a question about the statement, and five answer choices.

The typical length of the statement in each question is less than 100 words, shorter than Reading Comprehension passages. Occasionally there are two questions and answer choices following a single statement.

In this section we recommend that you read both the statement and the questions carefully and identify the assumption implicit in the statement with a heightened awareness of any weakness in the argument.

4.1 Fundamental Structure of an Argument

Premises/Evidence	- Clearly stated; Supporting facts or information or an observation or a conclusion based on a relevant situation - Can be inferred from assumptions and conclusion
↕ Assumptions	- Implicit; Unstated - Foundation of a conclusion - Sometimes there are no assumptions between evidence and conclusion - Can be inferred from evidence and conclusion
↕ **Conclusion (based on associated conditions)**	- Final decision deduced from assumptions and evidence - Different conditions to a conclusion can lead to different conclusions - Conclusion can be an entire sentence or part of a sentence

Example:

A student who scores high on the GRE usually scores high on the GMAT too. If Alice's GRE score is in the 99th percentile, she will score above 700 on the GMAT as well.

4.2   Type of Questions

There are four major types of questions. Among them, Assumption questions are the most common type. In particular, the Assumption – Weakening questions often times account for 40% of the total Critical Reasoning problems.

(1) **a) Assumption Questions**

   · **Assumption**

   · **Weakening**

   · **Strengthening**

   · **Flaw**

(2) **b) Inference/Conclusion Questions**

(3) **c) Paradox/Explain Questions**

(4) **d) Method of Reasoning Questions**

4.2.1 Assumption Questions

Assumption questions are the most common type of questions. Here you will normally see a conclusion in the statement along with some evidence supporting that conclusion. The question asks you to weaken or strengthen the argument, or to identify some unwritten assumption on which the argument relies, or some flaw.
These questions often also include

- **a proposal, plan or prediction**

- **comparison/analogy**

- **cause and effect arguments**

- **arguments about representative samples or numbers**

You can identify an assumption question because it will have the following words in the question:
– **ASSUMPTION** questions have *'assumption'*, *'which of the below is assumed by the argument above'*, or *'presumption'*
– **WEAKEN** questions have *'weaken'*, *'call into doubt'*, *'challenge'*, *'undermine'*
– **STRENGTHEN** questions have *'strengthen'*, *'which of the below best supports the argument above'* (compare this to the wording of inference and paradox questions)
– **FLAW** questions ask you to identify the *'flaw'* in the argument
These four sub-types of Assumption questions work in a similar way to one another.
i) Assumption Questions
Here you will normally see a conclusion in the statement along with some evidence supporting that conclusion. The question asks you to identify some unwritten assumption on which the argument relies. These questions often also include a proposal, plan or prediction, or feature cause and effect arguments or arguments about representativeness. You can identify an assumption question because it will have the following words in the question: 'assumption', 'which of the below is assumed by the argument above', or 'presumption'.
ii) Weaken Questions
These are the most common type of Critical Reasoning question. About 40% of all CR questions are 'weaken' questions. As with assumption questions, you will normally see a conclusion in the statement along with some evidence supporting that conclusion. The question asks you to identify the answer choice which contradicts or calls into doubt the conclusion of the argument. These questions often also include a proposal, plan or prediction, or feature cause and effect arguments or arguments about representativeness. You can identify a weaken question because it contains the words 'weaken', 'call into doubt', 'challenge', or 'undermine'.
iii) Strengthen Questions
As with assumption questions, you will normally see a conclusion in the statement along with some evidence supporting that conclusion. The question asks you to identify the answer choice which most clearly supports the conclusion of the argument. These questions often also include a proposal, plan or prediction, or feature cause and effect

arguments or arguments about representativeness. You can identify a strengthen question because it contains the words 'strengthen' or 'which of the below best supports the argument above' (compare this to the wording of inference and paradox questions).

iv) Flaw Questions

As with assumption questions, you will normally see a conclusion in the statement along with some evidence supporting that conclusion. The question asks you to identify a logical problem with the argument. It is not based on missing evidence, or an unwarranted assumption; instead it is based on drawing the wrong conclusionÑone that is too broad, or which confuses quantities (saying for example that if 'many' people believe something, then 'most' people hold that belief.) These questions often also include a proposal, plan or prediction, or feature cause and effect arguments or arguments about representativeness. You can identify a flaw question because it asks you to identify the flaw in the argument.

4.2.2   Inference/Conclusion Questions

Inference/Conclusion questions can be identified easily.

They have one or more of the words *'infer', 'inference', 'conclude', 'complete'* in the question. Inference questions contain a complete argument in the statement, and the question is asking you to find the answer choice which represents a possible conclusion from the argument. (This is **very** different from the other question types, where typically the conclusion is contained in the statement.)

Another common question wording for inference questions is *'which of the answers* **below** *is best supported by the statement* **above?***'*

4.2.3   Paradox or 'Explain' Questions

Paradox questions present you with two facts that appear to contradict one another. They have the words *'paradox'* or *'reconcile'* in their question; another common question which indicates the Paradox type question is 'which of the answers below best explains the above.' (Notice the slight but important difference from Inference questions).

The question is asking you to explain why the seemingly contradictory facts don't contradict each other.

4.2.4   Method of Reasoning Questions (MOR)

Method of Reasoning questions ask you to identify some structural feature of the argument in the statement. Occasionally these questions ask you to identify the function in the argument as a whole of some feature of the argument that is in **bold face**.

4.3   How to Tackle

With every question, **the place to start is with the question, not** the statement. You will come to recognize that there are a limited number of types of question, and understanding the question being asked before you read the statement means:

– you will clearly identify the type of question being asked
– you will read the statement with a clear understanding of what you are 'looking for' in the statement (for example, you may be looking for a way to "weaken" or "support" the argument made in the statement)
– you will be able to identify the best strategy for finding the answer.
In sum:

- **Step 1: Start with the question.**

- **Step 2: Identify the question type.**

- **Step 3: Identify the conclusion and then the rest of the argument structure. Diagram and Jot down keywords.**

- **Step 4: Focus on the statement. Provide your own answer.**

- **Step 5: Watch for trap answer choices. Select the right answer.**

In more detail:
You should approach questions of this type in the following way:

4.3.1   Start with the question

You should read the question first, before you approach the statement (even though the question is written after the statement on the page). This allows you to subsequently focus your reading of the statement towards the more important parts of it.
Tip: Do **not** assume what you will be asked about the argument without reading the question CAREFULLY. Even though some arguments may have a very serious flaw, the test-maker often tries to mislead you into identifying such an 'obvious' problem, when **in fact** the question is really asking you to identify a different and more subtle issue.

4.3.2   Identify the question type

As mentioned before, the main question types are:

(1) **a) Assumption Questions**

- **Assumption**
- **Weakening**
- **Strengthening**
- **Flaw**

(2) **b) Inference/Conclusion Questions**

(3) **c) Paradox/Explain Questions**

(4) **d) Method of Reasoning Questions**

The main argument types include:

- a proposal, plan or prediction

- comparison/analogy

- cause and effect arguments

- arguments about representative samples or numbers

4.3.3 Identify the conclusion and then the rest of the argument structure

Each argument can be broken down into its assumptions, its line of argumentation, its supporting observations, and its conclusion.

You have to clearly identify all parts of the argument. First, you should identify the conclusion. That way you can quickly understand what the argument is about.

Conclusion can be an entire sentence or just part of a sentence.

The possible positions of a conclusion include:

- In the end of the statement after assumptions and premises/evidence (most frequently)

- In the middle of the statement after some premises/evidence (occasionally)

- In the beginning of the statement before assumptions and premises/evidence (once in a while)

- In the answer choices (for Inference question types)

Signals:

> Accordingly
> As a result
> Consequently
> Hence
> Indicates
> It follows that
> So
> Should
> Suggests
> Therefore
> Thus

Additional Signals:

A strong disapproval or approval tone in a sentence, such as "quite foolish", "certainly increase..."

Then it is very important to detect the hidden assumptions, without which the conclusion would fail. For example, if the argument builds on a poll, the assumption is made that the poll is representative, which may not be the case (refer to insufficient sample size or biased sample fallacies mentioned earlier in the AWA section).

Lastly you need to examine how well the conclusion is supported by the evidence. Often time assumptions can be correct, but the line of logic is wrong in using the selected evidence to reach the desired conclusion.

The main evidence types include:

- Directly Relevant Factual Data

- Extrapolated Information based on Factual Data and Assumptions

4.3.4 Focus on the statement. Provide your own answer.

Based on the question type, identify the important 'parts of the statement' and for a moment, think about the answer to the question without reading the choices. Then use your own answer as a guideline or a process of elimination to identify the likely correct answer choice.

a) Assumption Questions

Here the key step is to identify the **conclusion**, which (unlike in the Inference questions) is contained in the statement. The questions can be especially subtle among Assumption questionsÑso make sure you have read and understood **precisely** what the question is asking.

As mentioned before, typically, the Assumption questions will fall into two key categories:

(a) **How to strengthen the argument** When you are asked what findings would strengthen the argument, you have to think about one hidden assumption which is not yet proven or the discovery that the conclusion holds in another situation. Note that "strengthen" does not mean to prove rigorously; you should just look for further support of the argument.

(b) **How to weaken the argument** In this case you have to attack one stated or hidden assumption or the supporting evidence.

b) Inference/Conclusion Questions

When you see an inference question, you know you are looking at the evidence (or premises) of the argument and that one of the answer choices is a possible **conclusion** of the argument.

c) Paradox/Explain Questions

In a paradox question, you will be given two trends or facts in the statement. Identify these two trends or facts, because the correct answer will be one which **reconciles** the two trends together.

d) Method of Reasoning Questions Here there is no general rule for 'what to look for in the statement' Ñ though generally the question is asking you to break down the **structure** of the statement and describe the role of a component part.

4.3.5 Watch for traps. Select the right answer.

Read through the answer choices provided and use the answer grid to cross out obviously wrong choices. Typically three out of the five choices would support the opposite from what is being asked for or provide no relevant information at all. You should identify these answers first and cross them off. Of the remaining two, both will probably support what they are asked to support, but one will be much stronger than the other. Be very careful before making your final choice.

a) Assumption Questions

Trap One: Be aware of distracting answer choices designed not for the type of the question you are facing, instead for a completely different type of question.

Just as with Inference questions, the test-makers will try to tempt you to go for the 'wrong kind' of answerÑby presenting you with a "conclusion" of the argument presented in the statement in the answer choices, which might be right if the question was an Inference one, but which doesn't answer the question of an Assumption question. This is one of the reasons identifying the question type can be so helpful Ñ if you know you are looking for a 'strengthener' or a 'weakener' you shouldn't be tempted by a 'conclusion'.

Trap Two: Be aware of opposite answer choices which you should not get confused with and should stay away from.

The two most common question types are 'weakeners' and 'strengtheners' (up to 50% of the Critical Reasoning questions overall can be AssumptionÑWeaken.) The answer choices of a Weaken question will almost always include a strengthener and vice versa. Under test conditions it is amazing how often test-takers become confused and go for the opposite answer of the desired oneÑsince so much of the time the way to dismiss a wrong answer is to observe that it is completely irrelevant (see "out of scope" below), the diametrically opposite wrong answer at least has the fact that it is definitely relevant to the original statement going for itÑand (as in Inference questions trap 3, above) the correct answer can be 'disguised' by a bit of slightly obscure wording which encourages you to skip it.

This is one of the best reasons to start by reading the question, not the statement Ñ if you stay very clear in your mind as to whether you are seeking to weaken or strengthen the argument you will be likely to get it right.

Trap Three: Do not rely on generic facts. As a rule of thumb, a good attack on an underlying assumption is more than just one real-life counterexample.

b) Inference/Conclusion Questions

Trap One: Be aware of distracting answer choices designed not for the type of the question you are facing, instead for a completely different type of question.

Since the Assumption questions are the most common type of question, 'trap' answer choices for the less-common Inference questions can look like typical answers you expect to see in an assumption questionÑfor example something that contradicts the argument and would be the answer for a 'weaken' question. Bear in mind that the answer in an inference question has to be a conclusion.

Trap Two: Be aware that your final choice should only be based on the very arguments presented in the tested question, not some generic facts.

Inference questions ask you to draw a conclusionÑbut it MUST be a conclusion that is fully supported by the evidence in the question. You will often see conclusions which look convincing but which rely on your 'outside knowledge' rather than only on the facts given in the statement.

Trap Three: Stay away from answer choices that contain opinions. Do not choose any "nearly correct" answers.

Always avoid answer choices that contain opinions Ñ you're looking for something that must be true based on the given evidence.

Similarly, watch for words that slightly distort conclusions. For example, if a statement gives evidence that would support the answer choice 'some people don't base their purchasing decisions on price alone', a common trap answer will be 'most people don't base their purchasing decisions on price alone'. **Watching for the words 'most',**

'often', 'usually', 'few', 'none' or 'no', and 'all', along with any other qualifiers or intensifiers, and considering whether their use is REALLY supported by the evidence, can be a helpful technique.

It's common for the test-makers to combine a slightly distorted but 'nearly correct' answer like this with another answer choice that is hard to decipher, but once understood is obviously trueÑthe hope is that you'll scan the answer choices quickly and settle for the 'close' answer because nothing 'jumps out' at you.

c) Paradox/Explain Questions

Main Trap: Be aware that you need to compare both conclusions, not just one of them.

Since the question asks you to explain an apparent contradiction, the common trap answers distract you from the contradiction and focus you on just one of the two trends. Remember that the correct answer deals with BOTH of the trends or facts in the statement, and that an answer which simply explains what may seem the 'more puzzling' trend in isolation is not fully satisfying the requirement in a Paradox question.

d) Method of Reasoning Questions

Main Trap: Do not choose any "nearly correct" answers.

Much like Trap 3 under Inference questions, the trap wrong answers in MOR questions give you a slight distortion of the correct answer. Again, watch for qualifiers and intensifiers and consider whether their use is correct.

4.4 Special Advice

- Be familiar with major critical reasoning questions category.

- Determine how the question fits into the main types.

    - Watch out for EXCEPT and LEAST
    - Look out for Signal Words

- Diagram the structure and Jot down key words

- "Pre-phrasing" your answer

- Identify distracting answer choices

    - Irrelevant/Out of scope
    - Focus on presented facts, not 'new information'
    - Use answer grids and cross off each wrong choice

Student Notes:

Chapter 5

Reading Comprehension

Reading Comprehension constitutes about one-third of the 41 Verbal questions. You may see as many as 4 passages in this section up to 450 words in each passage, followed by 3 or 4 interpretive, applied, and inferential questions.

The GMAT Reading Comprehension is a speed-reading exercise with relevant questions. It measures your ability to speed read, understand, analyze, and apply information and concepts presented in written English. Specifically, it evaluates your ability to:

- Understand words, terms and statements

- Understand the ideas, concepts and logical relationships between significant perspectives and to evaluate the importance of arguments

- Draw inferences from facts and statements

- Understand and follow the development of quantitative concepts as presented. Then interpret and use the data to reach conclusions.

As the GMAT is administered as a CAT and all three categories of verbal questions are intermingled, the first three or four questions you may face in the Verbal section may be Reading Comprehension. Unlike the random mix of Sentence Correction and Critical Reasoning questions, a short series of Reading Comprehension questions is presented consecutively in a group.

5.1 Key Facts

The topics in Reading Comprehension are typically related to social sciences such as politics and history, physical or biological sciences such as geology and astronomy, business-related areas such as marketing, economics and human resource management, along with other advanced subjects. Because the Reading Comprehension section includes passages from various different content areas, you may have general knowledge about some of the topics. All questions are to be answered on the basis of what is stated or implied in the reading material. Though no specific familiarity of the material is required, if you regularly read articles of broad topics, you will be at a slight advantage and be more confident.

Since it is particularly important to get the first few questions right, a great deal may be dependent on your understanding of a Reading Comprehension passage if it comes up first. Please also note that unlike the old paper-and-pencil GMAT, in a CAT, you will see only one question at a time. Therefore you can no longer apply the approach of going through all the questions first and reading the passage with the questions in mind.

Bear in mind that you have only an average of 110 seconds available for each Verbal question! This means you have just over seven minutes to read one passage and answer a group of four questions – not a long time. As mentioned earlier in Sentence Correction, Manhattan Review recommends you to bank some extra time for the Reading Comprehension section by completing Sentence Correction questions a little bit faster.

There is only one way to become proficient with the GMAT Reading Comprehension exercise – you must practice with all the material you can get your hands on!

5.2   How to Tackle

Here are some useful points for dealing with Reading Comprehension in the GMAT:

Identify the structure

After you understand what the text is about by scanning the first question and reading the first and last sentences and/or paragraphs, try to identify its structure while you are reading. That means that you should get a feel for how the paragraphs are structured together. The typical categories include:

- Supporting example

- Discussion of a counter argument

- Thesis-antithesis-synthesis

- Evidence-analysis-conclusion

- Change of direction, change of emphasis or introduction of new material, signaled with transitional "flags" such as: but, however, alternatively, furthermore, despite, on the other hand.

Effective note-keeping

You do not need to memorize every single detail. The goal is to be able to pinpoint the location where specific information is to be found later, not to retain the information in your memory. You may stop after each paragraph and briefly note on your scrap paper how it fits into the context of the passage, thus building up a list of a few key words that will allow you to rapidly find a particular reference in the passage.

Paraphrase Internally

As you are reading the introduction and body paragraphs, try to mentally recap each main point in very simple language. Some people find it helpful to ask themselves after every sentence "What was the point of saying that?" In this kind of writing, where a case is being constructed and argued, every sentence should "carry some water". If you find it effective, jot down a few key words. The purpose of this technique is to make sure you are grasping the essential information and messages being imparted, instead of being diverted or confused by florid language or unfamiliar constructions. Imagine that you must explain the paragraph succinctly to a child.

Consider answers to the generic question types

While reading, make it your second nature to come up answers for generic questions such as main idea, topic, purpose, structure, tone and conclusions. These questions do recur often in Reading Comprehension. Meantime, knowing those answers while reading through does help you deepen your understanding very effectively. That way you can save more time for content-specific questions (which often start "according to the passage...") to go back to check the source. The following shows how to deal with two typical questions.

- **Think of a suitable title for the passage**

  This is a common question in the GMAT. Also, this will help you determine the "boundaries" or scope of the subject matter under discussion, which relates to another common question, concerning the author's overall scope. When asked about the author's scope, main point, or area of interest, **choose an answer that encompasses as much of the passage as possible**, rather than a subsidiary point that may have been addressed in one or two paragraphs.

- **Determine the author's attitude**

  A common question concerns the author's attitude to the matters he is describing. As with the GMAT as a whole, strongly worded text is not favored, so **be cautious of extreme words** (e.g. "disgusted"). Observing convention, there should be even less emotional content in science and engineering passages.

- **Determine the author's likely conclusion**

  You may also be asked to identify which statement that the author would be most likely to agree. Remember that you are being asked to put yourself in the author's shoes, and that he might draw a broad general conclusion from the restricted and specific subject matter of his analysis.

Watch out for Negation questions

One of the most common mistakes made by test-takers is that they overlook Negation questions, which is surprisingly easy to do under the stress of the exam. Negation questions look for an answer which is unsupported or contradicted by the passage. A good way of spotting that you may have fallen into a Negation trap is if you find that more than one answer appears to be correct. In a Negation question, four of the answers will be supported by the passage, and you should be looking for the "odd man out".

Be objective & draw your conclusions based on provided text Stay within the confines of the passage; do not be tempted to incorporate your judgment, opinions or external knowledge. You are being tested on your abilities as an analyst, and so should restrict yourself to a literal interpretation of the words in the passage.

Look up the information asked

When you answer a question, always refer to the text. You are asked for specific details from the text and are often presented with intentionally misleading answers that ostensibly fit, so you must go back to the source. Do not rely on your recollection of the passage, which will begin to drift immediately after you have finished reading. Get into the habit of tying your answers back to specific wording in the passage, justifying each word in an answer choice.

Use the Process of Elimination

Process of Elimination is useful for Reading Comprehension questions. Answer choices can often be rapidly weeded out for being: too specific, too broad, too extreme, contradictory of the passage, or off-topic.

5.3   General Guidelines

To recap, we recommend the following general guidelines:

- Quickly scan the first question to understand the underlying topic. Read the first and last sentences and/or paragraphs particularly carefully.

- Read the passage in detail. Jot down key words.

- Note its main structure, scope, tone and conclusion.

- Pay special attention to the usage of transitional words that change the passage's flow, such as yet, though, however, despite, etc. These transitional words often highlight important information in the passage.

- Note different perspectives presented and the relationship amongst them.

- Quickly scan through the question and answers to develop a general sense of the focus of the question.

- Read the answers to note the possibilities addressed. At this point eliminate any clearly wrong answers.

5.4   Special Advice

The main challenge posed by Reading Comprehension is the turgid and technical nature of the material. The passages are usually written in a convoluted style and often contain abstruse content matter, typically of a specialized scientific, social science or business nature – passages of each type appearing with approximately equal frequency.

Learn from the Speed Readers

You can read much faster when you guide your eyes. Unfortunately, that is easier to accomplish on paper than it is on the screen. Nevertheless, you should try various techniques during your preparation until you find the one which you like the best. For example, you can guide your eyes by the pencil provided by the test center, or you can use the mouse pointer. Generally, there is no patent recipe, so you have to experiment.

Do not be over-concerned with technical language

GMAT does not test domain expertise. Instead, it is testing your ability to see patterns of information. For particularly esoteric material – for instance biochemistry – you may find it helpful to substitute generic labels such as "item A" for complex terminology, in order to better resolve the relationships and linkages that lie underneath the confusing surface camouflage.

Do not be daunted by an unknown word

Similarly, do not worry if you do not know the meaning of a particular word: 100% vocabulary is not a prerequisite, and often time people find that their best guess concerning an unknown word is more than adequate. However, a great grasp of a large English vocabulary can always be more helpful when you are aiming for a top score. To assist you in the process, please carefully review and study Manhattan Review's internally developed extensive GMAT Vocabulary List.

Find your own best navigation method

There are a few recommended techniques. However, practice and find the one or the combination that suits you the best.

Read the first question (questions appear on screen to right of the passage) before you read the passage itself. Some people find that they can concentrate better on the passage if they are actively seeking information, even on the first pass.

Read the first sentence and/or paragraph - which should set the scene - and then read the last sentence and/or paragraph. The introductory paragraph is the most important paragraph for understanding the whole text. Read it carefully, so that you understand the context in which the text is written. Move to the last paragraph, which, in a well-written text, should present the conclusion. Then go back to the beginning, with a clearer idea of what the passage is about.

Read more quickly through the remaining parts (but not so fast that you start skimming). **Please note that multiple re-readings of the passage waste a dangerous amount of time. Aim to read through the passage once and thoroughly.**

Read more carefully in your daily life

Though skimming is normal and adequate in daily reading, it will be more beneficial to you if you try to stop skimming and start to read each article more carefully. It is similar to practicing running with weights. From now until right before you take the GMAT, whether a book, newspaper or email from Human Resources, read it deliberately and absorb every word; this will require a slower reading pace. You just need to be more demanding on yourself when preparing for the GMAT and require yourself to be thorough and to focus your attention on all the information contained in a passage. As you improve your reading comprehension speed and the quality of understanding in general, you may use different techniques on the practice and actual tests. As mentioned earlier, multiple re-readings of the passage waste a dangerous amount of time. Aim to read through the passage once and thoroughly.

Student Notes:

Chapter 6

Analytical Writing Assessment

6.1 Your task

In this part of the test you must write two essays about topics that are presented to you. The CAT test program selects the questions randomly from its database of 90 issue questions and 90 argument questions. The order in which the issue and argument questions appear is also chosen by random. You will type the answers directly into the computer using a simple word processor built into the test software. You should get used to its functions before the actual test by training with the GMATPrep Software which uses the original software. You have 30 minutes to write each essay. You have to work on each essay separately and are not allowed to return to an essay once you have moved on or your time has expired.

6.2 Scoring Procedure

Your essays used to be evaluated by four different readers of whom two read and scored your issue and two your argument essay. All evaluation is done independently of the other readers and according to the scoring criteria provided by ETS. The grading is done by College and University faculty members from various subject-matter areas, including management education. Each reader grades the essay on an integer scale from 0 to 6. The final AWA score is the average of those four grades. In case the average ends with 0.25 or 0.75, your score is rounded up by 0.25 so that all grades are on a half point scale.

Since March 1999 a new procedure has been in place. Only one human reader evaluates each essay, and the second reader is a computer. In the case that the human reader and the computer agree on a grade, that grade stands. In the case that their grades differ, a second human reader will also score the essay.

Student Notes:

6.3   Evaluation Criteria

To determine the grade for your essay, the human reader will assess four areas of ability:

- **Substance**
  Your ability to write a persuasive and conclusive essay, including the exploration of relevant ideas and development of a sound position

- **Organization**
  Your ability to structure your essay conclusively

- **Control of Language**
  Your ability to write an essay with appropriate word choice and a variable syntax

- **Grammar**
  Your ability to write your essay according to the grammar and usage conventions of Standard Written English

Naturally, you should strive for perfection in all four areas. However, the substance and the organization of the essay may have more impact on the final evaluation than the other points, so you should be careful to focus on these points above all else.
Student Notes:

6.4   Writing Style

Although your writing style will not influence your score as much as organization and content, that does not mean it does not affect it at all. Apart from the obvious requirement that your essay has to be grammatically correct, it should be concise and show flexibility. The following points are worth mentioning to help you to achieve that:

- **Learn transitional phrases**
  You should build your own library of phrases, which can be used as building blocks. The ones we provide here can serve as a starting point.

- **Avoid sarcasm**
  Many people have adopted the habit of expressing their opinions through sarcastic remarks. In your AWA essay this will not be considered good style.

- **Avoid slang**
  Review your vocabulary to ensure it is Standard English. Often people get used to certain expressions, and do not remember that such expressions do not conform to Standard English. Use of slang will definitely decrease your AWA score.

- **Avoid fancy vocabulary**
  None of the graders will be impressed if you show that you have studied Latin for a few years or if you use the latest technical description of a computer chip. Make sure your essay is understandable to a normal educated person.

- **Reference correctly**
  When you discuss the argument refer to its source the first time you mention it. If no source is provided, refer to the 'statement' or 'claim'. In this way you avoid accidentally falling into to the trap of presenting your opinion on the issue. Generally, try to keep references to yourself to a minimum in the Analysis-of-an-Argument section.

Student Notes:

6.5   Analysis-of-an-Issue

6.5.1   The Question

In this part of the test you should present your opinion on a given topic in an effective and persuasive way. The question has two parts:

- Topic
  A short statement about an issue

- The Directive
  Instructions on how to respond to the statement made in the former part

The directions fall into roughly three categories:

(1) Discussion of the extent to which you agree with the statement

(2) Explaining your opinion of the correctness of the statement

(3) Explaining the meaning of the statement itself

While the latter two may be slightly more complicated to answer, your task can generally be described as taking a stand and providing reasons and examples to support it.

Student Notes:

6.5.2   The Structure of Your Essay

Since the presented topics allow for a wide range of options, there is no correct answer to the question. However, the following elements are always expected in your essay:

(1) An acknowledgement that the topic is complex to judge and allows for different points of view

(2) Your point of view on the topic

(3) At least two reasons to support your opinion

(4) At least two examples to support your opinion

Experience has shown that an answer of approximately 300 to 350 words is necessary to address all these issues in your essay. Your essay should have the following structure:

(1) Introduction

 · Reword the issue to be discussed
 · Acknowledge its complexity
 · State your position on the matter (without reasons)

(2) Body Paragraph 1

 · State your main reason why you support your position
 · Acknowledge a counterargument and refute it (optional)
 · Give one or two examples to support your reasoning

(3) Body Paragraph 2

 · State a secondary reason why you support your position
 · Acknowledge a counterargument and refute it (optional)
 · Give one or two examples to support your reasoning

 or alternatively:

 · Acknowledge a counterargument
 · Provide a rebuttal
 · Give one or two examples to support your reasoning

(4) Body Paragraph 3 (optional)

 · State another reason why you support your position
 · Acknowledge a counterargument and refute it (optional)
 · Give one or two examples to support your reasoning

 or alternatively:

 · Acknowledge a counterargument

· Provide a rebuttal

· Give one or two examples to support your reasoning

(5) Summary

· Restate your opinion

· Summarize the main points from the body paragraphs

Note that you do not have to follow this structure. However, given your task in this exercise, it makes sense to use it. On the following pages we provide a basic template for writing your essay. Of course, you do not need to adhere to our model strictly, as long as your essay is well-organized.

The following outline of the use of transitional phrases may serve as a first guideline on how to write this essay. Remember that you should adapt everything to suit your personal writing style:

(1) **Introduction** The question of whether or not ... depends on .... In my view, ...

(2) **Body 1** The main reason for my view is .... For example, ... Also, ... Finally, ...

(3) **Body 2** Another reason for my view is .... Specifically, ... Admittedly, ... However, ...

(4) **Body 3** Some might argue .... Yet .... Others might cite .... However, ...

(5) **Summary** In conclusion, I agree/disagree that .... However, ...; on the other hand ....

Student Notes:

6.5.3 Content

When writing your essay, keep in mind the following points, and avoid the following common mistakes:

- Start by brainstorming. When the question is given you should start by brainstorming for a couple of minutes and write down every argument and counterargument which comes to mind.

- Make sure you express an opinion on the subject. The issues can be argued either way; you may have a different opinion on the matter than the reader, but he will grade your essay *only* based on the way you present it. *There is no correct answer.*

- Keep in mind that you must acknowledge the other possible points of view on the issue and mention counterarguments. Leaving out any other view not supporting your position is not considered very persuasive by the ETS people. Naturally, after mentioning other possible views you should provide reasons why they are not too convincing.

- Avoid the appearance of being fanatical. The goal of the essay is to demonstrate that you are able to acknowledge different points of view and draw conclusions based on reason, not on a belief system written in stone.

- Be selective in your arguments. It is not possible to discuss the presented issues in great detail in the 30 minutes provided to write the essay. That is known to the graders, and they do not require a term paper for a full score. Just make sure you mention the best arguments and counterarguments from the brainstorming list you made at the beginning.

- Avoid excessive presentation of your technical knowledge. The same applies to personal experience, which is fine to some extent, but commonly known examples are preferable. No one will be impressed if you claim that you have seen a Yeti.

- Avoid mention of overused examples. When a reader comes across the same example for the hundredth time, he may not consider such an example very convincing. Hence you should avoid mention of Lady Di, Bill Gates and Adolph Hitler, etc. Use well-known but not overused examples like Steve Jobs instead of Bill Gates as the founder of an innovative computer company.

Student Notes:

6.6 Analysis-of-an-Argument

6.6.1 The Question

In this part of the test you should present your opinion on a given topic in an effective and persuasive way. The question has two parts:

- Topic
  A short line of reasoning is provided

- The Directive
  Instructions on how to analyze the topic

Your job here is not to present your own opinion, but critically to analyze the given argument.

6.6.2 The Structure of Your Essay

Again, your essay should range from approximately 300 to 350 words. We suggest the following structure:

(1) Introduction

  - Reword the argument to be discussed
  - Briefly sketch the argument's line of reasoning
  - Indicate that the argument has several logical flaws

(2) Body Paragraph 1

  - Pick your point of main criticism. This will be an assumption, a premise or a conclusion drawn at the train of thought
  - Acknowledge a counterargument and refute it (optional)
  - Strengthen your criticism by providing a similar point or an example

(3) Body Paragraph 2

  - Pick another point of criticism. This will be an assumption, a premise or a conclusion drawn at the train of thought
  - Acknowledge a counterargument and provide a rebuttal (optional)
  - Strengthen your criticism by providing a similar point or an example

(4) Body Paragraph 3 (optional)

  - Pick another point of criticism. This will be an assumption, a premise or a conclusion drawn at the train of thought
  - Acknowledge a counterargument and provide a rebuttal (optional)
  - Strengthen your criticism by providing a similar point or an example

(5) Summary

· Summarize your criticism of the argument

· Discuss how the argument could be improved and what points the author should have made to strengthen his case

As mentioned above, the following outline of the use of transitional phrases may serve as a first guideline on how to write this essay. Remember that you should be flexible:

(1) **Introduction** The author argues that ... because .... The author's line of reasoning is that, ... This argument is unconvincing for several reasons.

(2) **Body 1** First of all ... is based on the questionable assumption that .... However, ... Moreover, ...

(3) **Body 2** Secondly, the author assumes that .... However, ... It seems equally reasonable to assume that ....

(4) **Body 3** Finally, the author fails to consider .... For example, ... Because the author's argument lacks ....

(5) **Summary** In conclusion, to convince me that ..., the author would have to provide evidence that .... Without this additional evidence, I am not convinced that ....

Student Notes:

6.6.3 Content

The goal of this exercise is to recognize the logical flaws that are incorporated in the argument. Among the most common are the following:

- **Insufficient sample size**

  The line of argument draws conclusions from a small sample group about the whole population. That general derivation cannot be made without questioning or observing a larger number of test candidates. This fallacy could also be committed when the sample size is not mentioned in the argument.

- **Biased sample**

  To get representative data, random members of the population in question have to be selected and examined. In several arguments, a conclusion is drawn about the population without a statistically convincing selection. This fallacy and the former one are often found together.

- **False Analogy**

  This fallacy is committed, when conclusions are drawn simply on similarities in characteristics which may be uncorrelated with the characteristic that is derived. This conclusion is not valid in many of the arguments presented in the GMAT.

- **Defective Correlation**

  In many arguments, it is assumed that two events are correlated, simply because at some point they happened after each other. This may be a coincidence and does not allow further conclusions.

- **Insufficient Correlation**

  This is a weaker flaw than the previous point. Two events may be correlated, but there are several other factors which influence the appearance of the second event, too. Hence it cannot be concluded by the observation of one event that the other will appear with certainty.

- **Black-and-White Fallacy**

  In this argument, it is assumed that at some point only two options exist, one of which will undoubtedly appear. The flaw here lies in the fact that other outcomes may exist and cannot be ruled out.

When writing your essay remember that the arguments that are presented largely contain flaws. Your task is to find those flaws. Generally, you should disagree with the conclusion drawn, but suggest ways to improve the argument.

The most common mistake is to confuse both parts of the AWA. In this part you are *not* asked to present your own view; you should solely focus on the logical flaws in the argument.

Student Notes:

Chapter 7

Advanced Vocabulary List

The advanced vocabulary list is available as PDF-File.
Please email us at info@manhattanreview.com to request your free copy.